Twayne's United States Authors Series

EDITOR OF THIS VOLUME

Sylvia E. Bowman

Indiana University

Granville Hicks

TUSAS 387

Granville Hicks

GRANVILLE HICKS

By TERRY L. LONG
Ohio State University

TWAYNE PUBLISHERS
A DIVISION OF G. K. HALL & CO., BOSTON

Published in 1981 by Twayne Publishers,
A Division of G. K. Hall & Co.
All Rights Reserved

Printed on permanent/durable acid-free paper and bound
in the United States of America

First Printing

Library of Congress Cataloging in Publication Data

Long, Terry L
Granville Hicks

(Twayne's United States authors series ; TUSAS 387)
Bibliography: p. 166–69
Includes index.
1. Hicks, Granville, 1901–   —Criticism and interpretation.
PS3515.I253Z76   809   80–19870
ISBN 0–3057–7319–3

To Judy

Contents

About the Author

Terry Long has been interested in the literature and culture of twentieth-century America since his youth. This interest first led him into journalism; he worked on newspapers in Galveston and Corpus Christi, Texas, before becoming a college professor; and he still contributes occasional articles to newspapers in Ohio. The period of the Great Depression became his first scholarly passion; for the 1930s were a pivotal decade—one that saw the rise of fascism and of other radical politics, the New Deal, and the beginnings of World War II. Professor Long's readings about this somber, fervent decade led him to this study of Granville Hicks. While maintaining his interest in the 1930s, Professor Long has begun working on the cultural history of subsequent decades. At present, he is collecting oral history from industrial workers in Ohio. He feels that much of the untold cultural history of the last few decades needs to be preserved before it is beyond recovery.

Professor Long teaches literature and writing at the Ohio State University Newark Campus. He has also done industrial training in communications and has contributed as a volunteer to the media campaigns of political candidates whom he deemed honest and worthy. A native of Corpus Christi, he has B.A. and M.A. degrees from the University of Houston and a Ph.D. in English from Ohio State University. He has also taught at Texas A & M University and at Miami University (Ohio).

Preface

Granville Hicks, who wrote about American literature for fifty years, also commented about aspects of our society. As a dedicated literary critic, but also as a novelist, editor, teacher, and social thinker, Hicks was deeply absorbed in America's intellectual movements of the twentieth century. Hicks is significant for his radicalism of the 1930s, his liberal anti-communism of later years, his interest in the small town in America, and his devotion to criticism of novels written since World War II. This study is an attempt to describe, analyze, and evaluate his contribution in all these areas until 1977 when he quit writing.

Chapter 1 summarizes his career and the facts of his life and early influences. Chapter 2 covers his pre-Marxist years of critical writing, 1927–1931. Chapter 3 discusses his conversion to the Communist ideology in 1932 and his social and political philosophy (including his notion of the role of literature in revolution) until 1939, when he resigned publicly from the Communist party. Chapter 4 analyzes and evaluates his attempt to forge a Marxist critical method during these years. Chapter 5 discusses his disillusionment with communism and Marxist criticism and his social views as an ex-communist liberal.

Chapter 6 covers his four novels, his many essays, and his non-fiction book *Small Town*, all of which are concerned with his portrayal of—and preference for—life in small towns. Chapter 7 describes his gradual active return in the 1940s to literary criticism when he was beginning to contribute some of his best work about recent fiction. Chapter 8 surveys his eleven triumphant years as a book columnist for the *Saturday Review*, as well as his subsequent work since retirement from that magazine in 1969. Finally, chapter 9 makes an assessment of his contribution to American literature.

Since I have emphasized the career of Granville Hicks and not the authors he wrote about, I have not attempted to gather all of his criticism of one particular author in one chapter. The long career of Hicks went through several phases. Within each phase of his career, however, I have gathered together the comments he made about several authors. The reader who wishes to find what Hicks said about William Faulkner or Ernest Hemingway may consult, therefore, the index and easily locate the places in the book devoted to each. However, I have not attempted to correct Hicks about every assessment he ever made of our authors, even of the major ones. I have analyzed his criticism throughout the book, with ample illustrations and general evaluations. But a comprehensive evaluation of the fifty-year career of a literary critic would be a greater task than one book could encompass.

I have quoted from and summarized dozens of essays and reviews by Hicks in the process of analyzing his works. I have not, however, treated any one of his essays or reviews as a literary work in itself; for a detailed rhetorical or stylistic analysis did not seem fruitful. I do, however, make a general assessment of his writing style in chapter 9.

Although Hicks published many books, he wrote hundreds of magazine pieces that are an important part of his body of work. I have therefore given his periodical writings a great deal of attention by devoting two whole chapters to his book columns of the 1950s, 1960s, and 1970s. He started writing for magazines, and in them he made his mark. Indeed, of the many articles that Hicks wrote, I have chosen several dozen to discuss because they illustrate various aspects of his ideas and methods. As a result, virtually every periodical essay of importance is covered. Every book Hicks wrote is discussed, but his biography of John Reed, his early book on Christian theology, and some collections he edited are only touched upon briefly. Furthermore, every important aspect of his career is surveyed, with the exception of his work as a publisher's reader, his radio work, and his teaching—aspects of his career which are overshadowed by his literary contributions. This book should be very useful to anyone who wishes to know what Granville Hicks was about during his long career. For scholars doing studies of more special kinds, the book should provide a helpful foundation.

I am indebted to Professor John M. Muste of Ohio State University for his criticism and encouragement of this study. And I owe thanks to Robert A. Barnes, Dean of the Newark Campus of Ohio State, for seeing that I received clerical assistance; to members of the Newark Campus staff for preparing the

Preface

manuscript, especially Harriet Frazier and Patsy Heft; and to James F. Loucks, Associate Dean of the Newark Campus, for his help and encouragement.

TERRY L. LONG

The Ohio State University, Newark Campus

Acknowledgments

I am very grateful to Granville Hicks for permission to quote from his published works, and to his publishers as follows: to Macmillan Publishing Co., Incorporated, New York, to quote from *Small Town*, by Granville Hicks; to Harper & Row Publishers, Incorporated, New York, to quote from the Hicks Introduction to *Wright Morris: A Reader*, by Wright Morris; to *Saturday Review* magazine, New York, to quote from his many articles; to American Airlines, to quote from the *American Way* magazine book columns by Hicks.

Chronology

1901   Granville Hicks born September 9, in Exeter, New Hampshire, second child of Frank Stevens Hicks, and Carrie Weston (Horne) Hicks.

1919   Graduates from public high school in Framingham, Massachusetts. Enters Harvard College.

1920   Turns to activities in the Universalist Church in Framingham, including the church newspaper.

1921   Moves into a dormitory and joins Harvard Liberal Club.

1923   Graduates from Harvard *summa cum laude*. Enrolls in Harvard Theological School.

1925   Marries Dorothy Dyer. Decides to give up idea of being a Universalist minister and to teach and write instead. Becomes instructor in religion and English at Smith College, Northampton, Massachusetts. Meets Newton Arvin at Smith.

1926   Daughter Stephanie born. Comes under influence of Van Wyck Brooks and his ideas of the role of the artist in society.

1927   "The Parsons and the War" appears in the *American Mercury*. Disillusioned by the execution of Sacco and Vanzetti.

1928   *Eight Ways of Looking at Christianity*. Articles in *American Mercury, Forum, American Literature, New Republic*, and *Nation* magazines. Does reviewing, ghost writing, editing, and literary essays.

1929   Receives M.A. in English from Harvard. Assistant professor in English at Rensselaer Polytechnic Institute in Troy, New York. "Industry and the Imagination" appears in the *South Atlantic Quarterly*.

1931   Becomes a publisher's reader for Macmillan, a job he continues for more than thirty years.

1932   Buys country house on forty acres near Grafton, New York, where he spends summers. September, contributes to forum "How I Came to Communism" in *New Masses*.

1933   *The Great Tradition: An Interpretation of American Literature Since the Civil War.* "The Crisis in American Criticism" and other articles in *New Masses.*

1934   January 2, becomes literary editor of weekly *New Masses.* January, "The Social Interpretation of Literature" in *Progressive Education.*

1935   April, participates in American Writer's Congress. Fired from Rensselaer; moves to country home in Grafton. Revises edition *The Great Tradition.* Becomes member of American Communist party.

1936   *John Reed: The Making of a Revolutionary.*

1938   *I Like America.*

1939   *Figures of Transition: A Study of British Literature at the End of the Nineteenth Century.* Stunned by August 22 announcement of Stalin's pact with Hitler. October 4, "On Leaving the Communist Party" in the *New Republic.*

1940   *The First to Awaken.* "The Failure of Left Criticism." "The Fighting Decade." "The Blind Alley of Marxism."

1942   *Only One Storm.*

1944   *Behold Trouble.*

1946   *Small Town.* "The Spectre That Haunts the World" in *Harper's.*

1949   Begins frequent book reviewing for the *New Leader.*

1952   *There Was a Man in Our Town.* First "Living with Books" column for the *New Leader*, December 1, appearing every other week.

1954   *Where We Came Out.*

1958   March 24, last "Living with Books" column in the *New Leader*; April 5, first "Literary Horizons" column in the *Saturday Review.*

1965   *Part of the Truth* (autobiography).

1969   May 24, last "Literary Horizons" column for the *Saturday Review.* Spends six weeks in Europe, joining Wright Morris in Venice. Thereafter, writes occasional reviews.

1970   *Literary Horizons* (collection of reviews).

1973   July, first monthly book column for the *American Way* (published by American Airlines).

1974   *Granville Hicks in the New Masses* (collection of his writings from the 1930s).

1977   Stops writing altogether in January because of illness.

CHAPTER 1

Reflector of His Times

ON any day over a period of forty years, a visitor to the shabby little settlement of Grafton, New York, might have seen Granville Hicks enter the general store. To the visitor, this unpretentiously dressed man with spectacles could have been distinguished from his fellow townsmen only by the large amounts of mail he would have carried away. In fact, little would have indicated that Hicks was a man with an interesting literary career. Nor would our visitor have thought that Hicks—author, editor, teacher, and literary critic—was in many ways a microcosm of America's intellectual history of the middle of the twentieth century.

As he worked steadily year after year in his very modest country home near the Vermont border, Hicks chronicled the unfolding of our literature while he struggled with some of the main intellectual issues of our time: the impact of industrialism, the problem of moral values in a secular age, the search for community in a mass culture, and the relevance of radical politics to the quest for justice. Hicks seldom frequented the circles of the up-to-date New York literati; nevertheless, from his unlikely habitat he served as a reflector of his times.

I Background and Early Influences

Three influences shaped the young Granville Hicks and set his career in motion: his New England upbringing and religion, his early experiences with colleges, and the intellectual magazines that excited him and interested him in literature. These influences indicate a steady progression and, in retrospect, a logical one toward his adventures with radicalism, his disappointment with it, and his intellectual interests and views in later life.

The first influence, that of New England, is in every fiber of the man. Hicks was born on September 9, 1901, in Exeter, New Hamp-

15

shire. His father, Frank Stevens Hicks, was born in Boston, but
his family had roots in Maine. His mother, Carrie Weston
(Horne) Hicks, was also born in Boston, but her family came from
Cape Cod.[1] In Exeter, Hicks's father was superintendent of a
small factory, and Hicks has recorded in his autobiography *Part
of the Truth* that the family looked upon its early years in that
town as ideal. The Hicks family had to move from Exeter when
Granville was seven, for his father had to find another job. When
the father had obtained a clerical position in Quincy, Massachusetts, he settled his family in a new suburb, Norfolk Downs,
that was only a few miles from Boston. While living in this bleak,
treeless area—the kind of new housing development that Hicks
later deplored in his defense of the well-established small
town—Hicks, who was clumsy and weak, was always at the
mercy of tougher boys. Because he was bored with school and also
because he was poor at athletics, he became a reader and a stamp
collector.[2]

In 1912, the family moved to Framingham, Massachusetts,
which Hicks considered to be a great improvement over Quincy
because of the trees, a small yard, the friendlier people, and the
woods nearby to play in (instead of a marsh). As Hicks later
observed, "On the very first day a man said hello to me in the
street, and I reported to my mother that Framingham was just
like Exeter. It wasn't, but it was a large improvement over Norfolk Downs."[3] Hicks disliked the depersonalization and the con-
gestion of cities which contrasted with the familiarity and pleas-
ant surroundings of the small town. During the 1940s he was to
write *The First to Awaken* (1940), *Only One Storm* (1942),
Behold Trouble (1944), and *There Was a Man in Our Town*
(1952), four novels that deal in part with what he knew of small-
town life and of the intellectuals who tried to live in them. He
also produced *Small Town* (1946), an informal nonfiction study
of Grafton.

Hicks later recognized, however, that his lower-middle-class
upbringing in small towns had been narrow and stodgy. His
parents had warned him against bad boys, and the "good" boys
with whom he associated came from thrifty, churchgoing
families. As Hicks relates, "When I was six or seven, I had been
shocked to learn that a favorite uncle not only was a Democrat
and Free Mason but drank beer and even whiskey. This was in-
credible, for my father was a Republican, an Odd Fellow, and a

total abstainer. At fourteen I could laugh at my naivete in suppos-
ing that Odd Fellows were good and Free Masons bad, but I was
still not quite sure about Democrats, and I had the gravest doubts
about men who drank beer."[4]

Hicks's parents, who were either Universalists or Unitarians,
depending on which church was available, were not overly
religious. What they really believed in was education: "In their
minds education was economically, socially, and morally im-
perative. It was the means of avoiding the insecurity and indig-
nity of manual labor, but it was also a path to self-fulfillment and
the good life."[5] Since they let young Granville know that they
would make any sacrifice for his education and that he was expected to do no less, he studied hard. The high school had a good
college preparatory course; and, although he said he was often
bored with the curriculum, he did well and was graduated as the
valedictorian of his class. Moreover, he had become interested in
school activities and had become a leader on the school paper, in
the Boy Scouts, and in the young people's society of the Universalist Church.[6]

His first experience with the second influence—colleges
—began in 1919. Hicks commuted to Harvard College, where he
studied hard but took no part in the social activities during his
first two years. Since he soon saw that he could not compete
socially at Harvard, he retained his association with the Universalist church in Framingham. He worked on a church paper, thus
making a little money; and he attended church conferences and
conventions. His teachers at Harvard, he later observed, had
little intellectual influence upon him during the first two years; in
fact, the hometown eccentric but well-educated Old Doc Kay,
who worked as a janitor, was perhaps the first person to talk to
the young man about unconventional ideas. To Hicks, "What
Old Doc Kay gave me was a sense of the intoxicating excitement
that could come from contact with ideas. Though the old man
may have been a little ridiculous, . . . his zeal for new ideas was
a valuable antidote to the caution and suspiciousness of my
middle-class environment."[7]

Hicks enjoyed Harvard more in his junior and senior years. For
one thing, he lived in a dormitory. But more important, according to him, was his joining the Harvard Liberal Club, which had
its own house, served lunches, and invited every dissenting person
who came through Cambridge to speak to its group. The speakers

were socialists, Communists, anarchists, Single Taxers, crusaders for civil liberties, advocates of birth control, prison reformers, vegetarians, nudists, trade-union organizers, and internationalists. As a result of hearing some of these lectures, Hicks became convinced of the evils of war, developed a general dissatisfaction with the status quo, and incurred during this period some beliefs that he later derisively described in *Small Town* as his trinity of "the scientific mind, the social mind, and the open mind."

This credo, especially the ideas of social awareness and open-mindedness, probably came largely from his connection with the Universalist and Unitarian churches; and the receptiveness to science is certainly compatible with Universalist thinking. Although he did not make clear the exact sources of his ideas, they seem consistent with his liberal church connections and the kinds of activities carried on by the Harvard Liberal Club. Hicks remarked also in *Small Town* that he was distressed to see how abstract his ideas had been in his days as "the young man as evangelist." But because he had worked during the summers in factories and had written sketches about the people he had known there, he was glad twenty years later that he "had not been wholly a slave of the printed page";[8] for such experiences had given him at least some connection with the real world of factory workers.

The moralist bent was obviously strong in him. After graduation from Harvard in 1923 ("*summa cum laude* and with highest honors in English"), Hicks had decided that he might want to teach English. At the same time, he was nagged by an evangelical calling and thought he might devote his life to liberal church work to develop a better life on this earth, not in the hereafter. As a result, he enrolled at the Harvard Theological School, where he studied for two more years before he decided that the liberal churches were not effective instruments for the improvement of society and that, at any rate, he was not suited to be a minister. In 1925, he accepted a position as an instructor in religion and English at Smith College in Northampton, Massachusetts. That summer, he married Dorothy Dyer, a girl with a similar New England background whom he had begun dating while in high school.[9]

At Smith College, Hicks lost more of his Yankee intellectual innocence and saw firsthand what academic snobbery could be. He wrote later that he discerned in the members of the faculty at Smith a pattern of ideas: they believed in science and reason, especially their own, as solutions of humanity's problems; they advocated free speech but had no faith in democratic rule by the people; and they felt they were a civilized minority. They expressed their defiance and indifference by drinking in spite of Prohibition laws, by tolerating violations of the marriage vows, by being supercilious toward all religion, by regarding politicians as rogues and patriotism as a joke, and by shocking less sophisticated people. At first, Hicks found these attitudes unattractive—as he did again in the 1940s when he felt uncomfortable about intellectual snobbishness. He admitted, however, that encountering the thought of his colleagues had been a benefit: "Under its influence I sloughed off a good deal of foolish prudishness, and I think I acquired a new facility in dealing with ideas, but it was a bad business, an almost grotesque exaggeration of the attitudes that isolate the intellectual from the rest of society."[10]

One person on the Smith faculty who did not adhere to such intellectuals' ideas was Newton Arvin, who became a lifelong friend of Hicks and who had an intellectual influence upon him. Arvin, who was more democratic and more concerned with social justice than with sophistication, took literature seriously. A socialist ideologically, Arvin was "full of bitterness against the business civilization we lived in." Arvin had been under the influence of Van Wyck Brooks, who had championed the ideal of the American artist and the creation of a society that would be compatible with artistry. Beginning in 1915 with *America's Coming-of-Age*, Brooks had talked about the pressures imposed on art by an industrial, commercial, mass-oriented society; and he had prompted other critics to examine the effects of these pressures on art. When Arvin urged Hicks to read Brooks's *Letters and Leadership* (1918) and *The Ordeal of Mark Twain* (1920), Hicks not only read them but was influenced by them: he too was to see America as a civilization that ruined the true artist.[11]

In 1927 a series of events that profoundly affected Hicks while he was still at Smith drew him further toward the intellectual's alienation from society. When he participated in the activities to get clemency for Sacco and Vanzetti, he was appalled by the public's rejection of any such proposals. The noisy behavior of the townspeople of Northampton at a public meeting about the case galvanized Hicks's conviction that the intellectuals were alienated from almost all the rest of the population and caused him to believe that no justice existed in a business civilization like America's. These events clenched his dissatisfaction with the status quo and logically led, with the economic collapse of 1929, to his becoming a radical.[12]

II *Ventures Into Literature*

The third influence in the formation of Hicks's career was generated by the magazines that encouraged his writing career and instilled in him his first passion for literature. His professors at Harvard had not excited Hicks about literature, he said, but the literary magazine articles and reviews had done so. These magazines rather than his educational experiences had motivated him to become a teacher and writer and had thus partly led him to Smith College. While teaching, he secured editing work and reviewed books for a newspaper. After Hicks published his first important piece (in 1927), an essay in the *American Mercury* entitled "The Parsons and the War,"[13] which demonstrated how hawkish and jingoistic the clergy had been during World War I, he was soon writing other essays and reviews for that publication as well as for the *Forum*, *American Literature*, the *New Republic*, and the *Nation*. In 1928 he published the fictional dialogue *Eight Ways of Looking at Christianity*, which was the result of his reading religious material. Hicks, who later dismissed the book as unoriginal, never considered it to be a work of piety, as it was later labeled by his enemies who knew only the title.[14]

As in the case of Hicks, the little magazines and intellectual journals have been important outlets for and influences upon American intellectuals. Such publications helped shape the modernist rebellion against the genteel traditions of the later nineteenth and early twentieth centuries. Periodicals like the *New Republic*, the *Nation*, *Sewanee Review*, the *Masses*, the *Liberator*, *Hound and Horn*, *New Masses*, the *Bookman*, the *American Mercury*, the *South Atlantic Quarterly*, *Partisan Review*, *Harper's*, the *New Leader*, and (to some extent) the *Saturday Review* gave Hicks and his fellows their intellectual stimulation. From the beginning, magazines were the outlets for Hicks's work. He built his reputation and his career by writing for them.

Hicks returned to Harvard for a year of graduate work in

English and received his master's degree in 1929. He had hoped to resume teaching at Smith; but, since his former position was not available, he became an assistant professor of English at Rensselaer Polytechnic Institute in Troy, New York. While studying at Harvard, Hicks had firmly decided that he did not want to do literary research, but he had also proved that he could do it by publishing some papers from his graduate courses. He continued to review books, to edit or ghostwrite others, and to write literary articles.[15] Although Hicks was establishing a point of view from which to criticize literature—basically that of a social moralist—and was gaining in knowledge and sophistication, he was still a prudish, earnest young man.

We might note that Hicks lacked the social and cultural advantages that other literary critics were given from birth. Edmund Wilson, for instance, enjoyed the support of a distinguished family background, European travel, excellent prep school training, exposure to the arts, and other amenities.[16] Hicks, on the other hand, was a plain Yankee from the lower middle class. Even his friend Malcolm Cowley, as Hicks pointed out in a conversation, had spent time in Paris from the early 1900s on, and had studied criticism and literature in France.[17] Some European exposure might have made Hicks more cosmopolitan, but he did very little traveling until late in life, and he was not well versed in European literature. When Hicks went to England in 1967 and to continental Europe in 1969,[18] these trips were the excursions of a man whose life's work was largely behind him, not the experiences of a young mind in formation. It appears that he was bound in by—but also strengthened by—his humble New England background and family life. While he had a limited cultural perspective, he may have benefitted, on the other hand, by being isolated from another influence: the pack mentality of the New York literary set (which is not necessarily cosmopolitan).

III   *A Home and a Way of Life*

At Rensselaer Polytechnic Institute, Hicks corrected his students' freshman papers; but he was more interested in his own writing. The significant thing about his position at Rensselaer was not the college so much as a related event, the purchase of a country home. After a year at Rensselaer, Hicks had hoped to move to a college teaching position more congenial than the one an engineering school provided. But the Depression had begun, other teaching jobs were hard to find, and Hicks and his wife Dorothy began to look for a country house, perhaps in nearby Vermont. When they found a one and a half story house on forty acres of land with trees and garden acreage in the spring of 1932, this property became the home place where Hicks established himself and a way of life. From the back screen porch, the Hicks family had a view of Vermont mountains—the Taconics, with Greylock in the distance—and they were near the village of Grafton, fifteen miles east of Troy.[19]

At first the Hickses spent only the summers in their country home, for they kept their rented house in Troy. By 1932, the Depression was deepening, Hicks was already involved in Marxist activities, and the capitalist system seemed to be on the verge of collapse. He was writing articles exploring Marxist approaches to literature, was active in a Communist study group, and was writing his book *The Great Tradition* (1933) about American literature since the Civil War. Following that book, he worked on his excellent biography, *John Reed: The Making of a Revolutionary* (1936), which was another result of his Marxist interests.

According to his autobiography, when Hicks returned from the Communist-sponsored first American Writer's Congress in April, 1935, he learned that he was not to be rehired by Rensselaer because he was a Communist—although the school denied that his political affiliation was the reason. As a result, Hicks established during that year the manner of living that he continued thereafter. He worked at home in the country and had weekend guests to supply his need for intellectual companionship. And among his many visitors over the years were professors, students, writers, journalists, editors, and others of an intellectual bent. Some steady friends and visitors were Daniel Aaron, historian; Richard M. Bennett, architect; Louis Birk, publisher; Henry Christman, journalist; Malcolm Cowley, literary critic and editor; Robert Gorham Davis, Newton Arvin, Harvey Curtis Webster, and Howard Doughty, English professors; Bernard Malamud and Wright Morris, novelists; Richard H. Rovere, Washington editor for the *New Yorker;* Edith H. Walton, magazine editor; and many other literary acquaintances. As the years passed, Hicks developed more contacts in the literary world, and one source of such contacts was Yaddo, a mansion in Sarasota Springs, New York, that had been endowed as a haven for writers and artists. His friend Arvin, who had been a director there for a long time, had asked Hicks to serve on a guest-selection committee; and Hicks became a director on the board of Yaddo in 1942. From time to time, beginning in 1969, he and Dorothy resided at Yaddo; and they managed it for a while.[20]

IV *Earning a Living on Literature*

Making a living as a man of letters has never been easy, and the usual ways have been either to write books that sell or to teach. Since Hicks was no longer a teacher, he turned to an opportunity that had become available to him in 1931 when H. S. Latham of the Macmillan Company had asked him to read manuscripts and to do some scouting. Since the search for writers had not developed, but the reading of manuscripts had, Hicks increased his reading for Macmillan; and this work became a source of income that lasted thirty years, during which time he submitted more than two thousand manuscript reports. Thus, his free-lancing and his manuscript reading became his primary sources of income. Much of the criticism that he wrote during the middle and later 1930s, however, was for the *New Masses,* and he received no pay for that work. He did have royalties from his books, and he did receive a Guggenheim Fellowship in 1935.

Although Hicks's life is interesting if for no other reason than that he found a compatible life-style by making his living as a free-lance writer and critic, his financial rewards were not high considering the arduous labors involved. He wrote over the years a few books of criticism and his already mentioned novels and biography, but the royalties were seldom high. At first, Macmillan paid him fifteen dollars for reading a manuscript; and, according to his own account, Hicks managed in the 1930s to earn about one hundred dollars a month this way. His starting salary at Rensselaer in 1929 had been $2,800; during the late 1930s, however, he was never able to make that much free-lancing; in fact, his annual income was one half to two thirds as much as it had been from his teaching position. But he had his home paid for, his thirty acres were used for a crop and garden, and his woods supplied him with fuel. And, of course, the purchasing power of the dollar was four or five times as high as now.

Other ways of earning money occurred from time to time. In August, 1941, for example, Hicks first appeared in "Speaking of

Books," a discussion show on radio in Schenectady. Later he became chairman of "Speaking of Books" and continued this program for a few years. In 1942 he was paid to take part in a conference on New England life that was sponsored by the Rockefeller Foundation; and two years later, when he received a grant from that foundation, he used the money to further his study of small town life, to read Arnold Toynbee's *Study of History*, and to write his book *Small Town* and some articles.

Until the late 1940s, when inflation really began, Hicks was able, he said, to live comfortably on the $5,000 or so a year he earned in that decade. In the 1940s and 1950s, seventy-five dollars was the highest one could expect from a scholarly journal for an article; and *Harper's*, *Forum*, and such magazines paid three hundred dollars or less. After World War II, the *New York Times* paid fifty dollars for a short review and one hundred dollars for a longer one. Other examples of the kind of work Hicks did to piece together a living were a yearly survey of American literature for an encyclopedia that paid fifty dollars and a series of annual reports about communism for an encyclopedia yearbook from 1946 through 1958.

But, when he sent his daughter Stephanie to Antioch College in 1943, he had to increase his income by accepting more work from Macmillan. Hicks had often thought that part-time teaching would help him keep up with inflation; however, colleges were reluctant in the early 1950s—the years of McCarthyism and the Cold War—to get involved with anyone who had been connected with communism. The fact that Hicks had resigned publicly from the Communist party in 1939 made little difference. But in September, 1955, Clara Mayer, dean of the unconventional New School for Social Research in New York City, asked Hicks to teach a seminar in novel writing. The pay was low; but, since the job took him to the city more often, it enabled him to meet and keep in touch with literary and publishing people.

In 1958, several opportunities suddenly opened for Hicks. That winter, Arvin hinted that Hicks might get a visiting position for a year at Smith College, and he soon received the offer. A while later, he received an important call from Norman Cousins, who asked him to contribute his book column to the *Saturday Review* rather than to the *New Leader*. The pay was to be substantially higher, and the column was to be a weekly one. That winter Hicks was also asked to teach the second semester of the following year at New York University. As a result of these developments, Hicks rejected the Smith appointment, kept the other teaching job, and started the *Saturday Review* column, which he named "Literary Horizons." Thereafter, Hicks served as visiting professor at numerous colleges in the East and Midwest. And after he began "Literary Horizons," he received many lecture invitations from universities. The usual rate in the late 1950s and early 1960s was five hundred dollars for a lecture, a considerable sum at that time. At the age of fifty-seven, then, Hicks had finally "arrived," and he still had some of his best work ahead of him.[21]

Probably one of our most productive critics, Hicks spent a large part of his life reading thoroughly four or more books a week for reviewing; meanwhile, he was occupied with a variety of other activities and was writing numerous articles. During his career, Hicks wrote at least fourteen hundred reviews and more than two hundred essays, not to mention fourteen books. As we have already observed, magazines were the primary outlets of his work and a source of inspiration to him. Clearly, the story of a literary journalist like Hicks is an interesting chapter in the cultural history of America.

CHAPTER 2

Early Criticism, 1927–1931

A S we noted in chapter 1, Hicks began to establish himself as a promising young critic with articles in magazines and journals in 1927. To the Hicks of these early five years of his career, literature was important for what it said about a society and its moral values. Hicks thus approached literature as a humanistic moralist, and he carried this moral bent with him into Marxism. He modified his philosophy, he changed his emphasis in literary judgments, but he retained many ideas established in this early period. A survey of the criticism of his early career demonstrates his interests and the principles he applied in judging literature.

I Literature and Values

Hicks insisted that values, the social principles or standards considered desirable for civilization, were the central concern of literature, or at least of literary criticism. In this regard, Hicks took issue in 1929 with Joseph Wood Krutch, who said that we had lost some helpful religious illusions with the coming of science—illusions that gave us a set of principles to live by. Hicks argued that such principles had been and could be created without religious notions such as divine revelation, a man-centered universe, and eternal reward and punishment in a life after death. He liked Krutch's *The Modern Temper*, however, for it helped to "shake us out of our present temper and into a mood which will discover new ways of stating old values and create fresh values for the future."[1] Presumably, Hicks was referring to the principles of social behavior, love, and justice that could be inculcated into humans without religion—or at least without religion that collided with science and with new social needs brought about by science, such as birth control, divorce, a new sexual morality, and new notions about economic justice.

In discussing some of the indecency of the literature of the

1920s, Hicks pointed out in 1928 that most writers expressed disgust with life and were searching for reality. Men seemed to have the material tools to build a new society, but they did not have a plan. To find such plans, men had to turn to those who could "perceive imaginatively the possibilities of the world that is," brush away old dogmas, such as those of religion, and affirm life. Such seekers had to accept alienated writers like James Joyce, Robinson Jeffers, Aldous Huxley, and Eugene O'Neill because only then could they "understand and accept whatever fresh affirmation of life they or their successors may develop."[2] Hicks liked a book by Irwin Edman, which he reviewed in 1929, because Edman was among those critics who were introducing a more positive feeling in social criticism. He felt Edman was right in trying to restate old values and discover new ones, and words like "values" appeared often in Hicks's essays and reviews of the time.[3]

Hicks also argued that social tendencies and literature were unavoidably connected. He agreed with E. E. Kellett that there was an "intimate relation between literature and philosophical, scientific, and political tendencies." To Hicks, Kellett's research answered those who scorned the attempt "to associate the desire for a flourishing literature with the effort for a better social order."[4] Because Hicks did not approve of a person's turning his back on society in the search for values to live by, he disapproved of Robert Graves in *Good-Bye to All That*. Graves was admitting defeat, Hicks said, by "taking refuge in some fancied realm outside of time and event."[5] Hicks could not conceive of anyone's not wanting to be concerned with the central issues of his own time.

One of these central issues, he argued, was modern man's adjustment to industrialism and his difficulty in maintaining humane standards in an age of machines. His essay "Industry and the Imagination" dealt in 1929 with the same theme he was later to study in his first important book *The Great Tradition* that, published four years later, presented the Marxist view of his subject. In the article, Hicks said that the artistic view of man could be more penetrating and unified than the scientific or utilitarian views. Although the writer needed to relate industry to life and human values, it was hard to choose the values intelligently. The writer should have a philosophy, but he need not and probably should not put it in a dialectic. He could not, however, have just any point of view: ". . . the number of valid and fruitful attitudes is limited . . . measured by the nature of art and the nature of the subject matter." The writer had to make an "imaginative assimilation" in his writing just as we do in real life (he did not explain what he meant). Novels could do more than protest; they could also show beauty in the life that industry shaped. Although such a literature might have to wait until men accepted industry the way their ancestors had accepted the sea and agriculture, an imaginative solution need not wait: the drift of events might become apparent to the perceptive artist who could "show forth imaginatively the way to a civilization that has learned to make industry its servant."[6] Of course, what Hicks wanted was a prophetic novelist who would show the way for the *future*, not just interpret the present or the past. Just what this central vision would be was not clear; what was clear was that Hicks expected the artist to have a comprehensive moral vision which he would bring to life in his works.

The search for values had to continue, but the churches did not seem to offer any hope to Hicks. Because of his background in religion, he was often asked to review books about it. A book on the faults of the Catholic church, he suggested in a 1929 review, would bring agreement from non-Catholics relative to the errors of the church; but they would not believe reform could be achieved. And, in reviewing three other books on religion in that same year, Hicks said that two were worthless and that the third one about the history of Christianity showed how little Christianity seemed to relate to modern life and how totally inadequate it was relative to social reform.[7]

To Hicks, the academic New Humanists led by Irving Babbitt and Paul Elmer More did not have a satisfactory answer. The Humanists, we might note, urged a return to the classical concept of humanity as distinct from God and nature. They opposed the idea of natural rights with the idea of humanistic and aristocratic democracy. They offered a classical and Christian view of moral and literary values; and they opposed naturalistic writers like H. L. Mencken, Theodore Dreiser, and John Dos Passos. The Humanists urged moral restraint in personal conduct and balance and moderation in aesthetics. They admitted that ethical self-control might be applied on the level of religion, and they speculated that their philosophy might create a new faith through a union of all faiths. Although the Humanists were right, Hicks said, in wanting to create standards upon which to judge literature, their standards did not meet human needs because they were not based on human nature but on a doctrine of divinity. Further, he said, the Humanists' rigid dualistic dogma (that religion and the world were distinct, as were mind and matter) drove them into the church. The human imagination's greatest achievement, Hicks argued, was not in showing the need for restraint but in the envisagement of purposes "toward which life may be guided and for the sake of which restraint is naturally and whole-heartedly exercised." Instead, the Humanists wanted to make literature "a series of pamphlets advocating the inner check." Babbitt and his followers had helped America guard against excessive romanticism and frivolous skepticism, but others had to go forward in an unexclusive, critical, open-minded search for values.[8]

Hicks conceded that the search for values led us directly to the problem of doubt—a problem which modern man had to resolve. In the past, when men had been confronted with change, they had tried resignation and abandonment of the struggle of taking part in their society. Men needed to find affirmation rather than withdrawal, but the affirmation, Hicks argued, had to be built on a firm foundation. In a review in 1930, Hicks observed that the two kinds of current affirmation being offered were Humanism and social radicalism, both of which he then rejected. The Humanists affirmed "individual development through the imitation of classical models and the exercise of the inner check." The social radicals asserted that a better social order was possible, and they argued that men should work strenuously for it. Both of these groups, said Hicks, ignored the fundamental metaphysical questions about man's relationship to his universe, such as the nature of death, creation, and a hereafter. They could do that for a while, and their values would work; but since the fundamental questions would return, "the only result of this temporary affirmativeness will be a deeper plunge into pessimism."[9]

Hicks did not explain what he meant by a firm metaphysical foundation for affirmation, nor did he pursue the idea elsewhere. Although he displayed resistance to radicalism, it was by this time no doubt entertaining his mind; for the economic collapse that caused the Depression had already begun. In any case, Marxism soon supplied Hicks with an answer to all such questions. Ironically enough, Hicks had predicted that such radicalism could produce pessimism if it failed; and, after 1939, that is what happened to him; for he suffered disillusionment and dislocation. And after a narrow Marxist concern with social ills during the 1930s, he returned in the 1940's and later to metaphysical questions, among others, as legitimate subjects of literature.

Values that were derived from the humane tradition rather than from any orthodoxy were important in literature, according to Hicks. The human values handed down from the traditions of civilization, not the accompanying illusions of supernatural revelation, he said, were what we should preserve and modify to meet the changing needs of modern civilization. And the imaginative artist was to play an important role in establishing these values.

II Literature and Society

Society, of course, was to benefit from the artist's assimilation of and portrayal of human values, but just how this benefit was to be conferred on society was an intriguing problem for the critic. Hicks addressed himself during his early career as a critic to the question of culture and the masses, and to the problem of social reform and the connection of literature with it.

In 1929 he stated an opinion concerning literature and the masses that is interesting in the light of what he later was to argue about proletarian literature. Although Herbert Read had argued that a modern poet could avoid sterility only by being close to his world and his people, poets like T. S. Eliot and Robert Frost, said Hicks, were achieving by exclusion and rejection a humanistic world to which they could respond. This process of excluding and rejecting much of humanity might have to continue until America had a culture related to, but not identical with, the culture of the masses.[10] A year later, with the Depression already taking its toll, Hicks showed again his interest in the problem of culture and the masses. He agreed with Matthew Josephson that the story of American writers was one of frustration because of our country's lack of tradition and its rapid growth. But we could not ignore social problems in order to develop culture; we could not have the benevolent Platonic state, nobly but absolutely led, that Josephson wanted. Although such a situation might develop, it could not do so until the machines had provided the material things for everyone. Even then, opined Hicks, questions about the culture of the masses might arise, for the masses probably would

not care for culture, but, if they had their bread and their cir-
cuses, an intelligent minority could cultivate and enjoy art—and
the masses could be exposed to and affected by such culture. We
had to create such a minority, he said, and we did not have to
wait for utopia to begin to do so.[11]

Thus, unlike the Humanists, Hicks advocated material well-
being for the masses as well as culture for the minority, but he did
not define his cultured minority as an esoteric group. This minority was to provide civilizing influences that the masses could draw
upon. Later as a Marxist, Hicks was to argue that revolutionary
writers had to address themselves *directly* to the masses and to
help create the new culture of the proletariat. The cultured
minority was later viewed by Hicks as *itself* the product of decay-
ing capitalism, and proletarian literature was to create a rebirth
of culture and civilization.

This shift from a belief in culture for the minority to the problems of the masses is reflected in what Hicks wrote during 1931,
the year of his transition from liberalism to communism. In that
year, he insisted on the importance of the political and economic
situation of society. As the Depression deepened, Hicks became
preoccupied with literature as a reflection of a sick society; and he
rejected more and more the writers who did not evince the moral
and social commitment that he felt was necessary. The new
writers expressed a sense of frustration, maladjustment, disintegration, or even disgust and defeat. "It is the old, old story in
American literature. A smudgy discontent, seldom breaking into
the clean blaze of tragedy, fills our literary life," he said. We
tried different solutions, but could not seem to find an answer.
"Can we much longer disagree with those diagnosticians who
regard our literature as the literature of a sick society . . . ?" he
asked.[12] Hicks's later answer to the writer's frustration was
revolution and an identification with the masses. The writers who
continued to deal in frustration rather than to hold out hope of
reform through revolution were later rejected by Hicks and condemned as bourgeois enemies of the masses.

III   *The Critic's Vocation*

Along with his concern for the artist's role of shaping values for
society, Hicks tried to formulate his ideas about the role of the
critic. Two statements he made in 1929 and two in 1932 represent

his thinking as a developing writer who was deciding to devote his life to criticism. The critic's function was "to focus all his resources on the book at hand, in order to illuminate not only the particular book but . . . life and literature." Even if the critics made mistakes, they should state their honest beliefs, Hicks said, because what counted was "the quality of intelligence and imagination behind the criticism, the power of clarification, the relating of knowledge and experience to the problem at hand."[13] Impressionistic criticism such as that of James Huneker had not been enough, Hicks argued, but neither was a criticism based on any dogmatic theory. Impressionism was based too much on emotions, and Humanism was too dogmatic. But there was in 1929 a "sharpening of perception, a struggle to create standards, an increased attention to the object of criticism instead of the feelings of the critic."[14] Hicks applauded this trend. He was soon, of course, to be caught up in another dogma, Marxism, though he would not call it that.

Early in 1932, when Hicks talked of the function of reviewers, he considered the relative goodness or badness of a book as stated by reviewers as not so important as the other items or aspects they discussed: "Their function is not to enable their readers to pigeonhole a book as good, bad, or indifferent; it is . . . to stimulate their readers, to sharpen their perceptions, to awaken their powers of appreciation, and to orient them in the living world of thought."[15] Hicks held throughout his career that reviews were to be written for readers; they were not published for those who avoided reading books but desired to be able to talk about them.

Hicks had more to say about the critic in a March, 1932, article, "The Dilemma of a Critic," which stated his feelings about criticism and his dedication to it as a vocation. To Hicks, the critic (meaning especially the reviewer) had to have another job since criticism did not pay enough, and since the critic never had time to read all he should have. Nonetheless, society needed "such cripples as we critics are. . . . If we do not resist the pressure of advertising and the menace of standardization, who will? Who else will expose the tricks of facile mediocrity and discover the virtures of the obscure and reticent innovator?" And who, he asked, would define the assumptions upon which the artist built, or rescue from dust the ignored achievements of the past? The critics did these things badly, but who would do them well? This article was unsigned, he explained, because he faced a personal problem of how to survive and be a critic; he knew no better way but to do double duty, to work at another job while also being a critic. The virtue and authority of criticism through the ages "have been won by men who made mind and body do double duty in order that they might be judged by standards that did not exist. . . ." Only if the critics did a good job would the standards and the criticism be what they should be. "Even such a hope is irrational, but it is the only thing I know of that I am quite sure I want to gamble my life on."[16]

The sense of dedication that Hicks had once thought to direct toward being a liberal church minister had shifted instead to criticism. And although he changed his opinions and his theories during the following decades, he maintained his basic dedication and his feeling about the importance of criticism.

IV *His Early Critical Method*

In this early part of his career, Hicks developed a set of premises and critical approaches which we can delineate. His critical method was grounded on the two ideas already discussed; that literature should reflect rationally held human values and that it had some connection with and effect upon society at large. Along with these attitudes were his tendency to discuss only in general terms matters of form and style, his emphasis on content, his set of ideas about the qualities the writer should have, and his interest in classifying types of novels and approaches to fiction. Some examples of his criticism in the pre-Marxist years demonstrate his critical method and interests.

A writer needed the "imaginative power" to create scenes and characters that seemed real, Hicks often said. In discussing Nathaniel Parker Willis (1806–1867) of Maine, for example, Hicks said he was a poet of "religious doggerel." His poetry showed little imaginative power, "and in his short stories, his novel, and his two plays there is not a character that comes to life."[17] Of Nathaniel Hawthorne, Hicks said that he failed to create "flesh-and-blood men and women" to express his important ideas, a flaw which was a "tragedy of isolation."[18] We can perhaps ignore his narrow view of Hawthorne when we read that, to Hicks, DuBose Heyward was good at depicting static characters and even in showing the changing society of Charleston, but he was not good in showing the development of character.[19] Hicks simply had not experienced enough literature to understand that Hawthorne was not interested in writing a middle-class novel of realism that depicts ordinary citizens living ordinary lives and that deals with human character and morality in a matter-of-fact rendering, for Hawthorne was writing symbolic and allegorical fiction. Although Hicks may have denied it, he was most interested in fictional realism. Hicks did not state very clearly what his criteria were; in such reviews as these, many of his comments were vague and general; but such vagueness is probably difficult to avoid since a reviewer has limited space. More often than not, what he said about a book was accurate, but his criticism often lacked the details that would have substantiated his generalizations.

Some comments that he made in 1929 on Ernest Hemingway showed, however, that Hicks was not oblivious to style. In *A Farewell to Arms*, Hemingway had strengthened his novel, Hicks said, by choosing words that were not worn from repetition. Love and war were made more moving because of this style: "By ripping away the verbal trappings supposedly appropriate to these subjects, he has gained, not lost, in poignancy. He has even had the courage to end the book with tragedy, and he has succeeded in conveying, not the grand and largely literary emotions theoretically associated with tragic loss, but a blankness and a bleakness far more terrible."[20]

Hicks did express some reservations about Hemingway in an article in 1930 that reflected his critical ideas. Both Hemingway's style and characters, Hicks said, showed that he did not trust conventional values. His characters who stood between two worlds surrendered much but preserved a bleak integrity. The Hemingway world, however, was not so representative as many admirers of Hemingway believed: "There are, as there always have been, other worlds than that which he has made his own, and now that he has utilized this one so effectively, one wishes he would turn to some other."[21]

Hicks believed that a writer had to know intimately what he was writing about; for, without this knowledge style and technique would go for naught. David Graham Phillips had been good at documenting his novels and in showing how men rose to success and how corruption worked. But Hicks conceded that the novelist needed also the ability "to fashion plausible, self-consistent, well-rounded characters" and that Phillips had not done so. However, "the stylists and technicians, the devotees of form and worshippers of the letter," did not do so well because they lacked the kind of knowledge of America that Phillips had had.[22] Although Hicks talked about "imaginative power" and the "ability to create living characters," he still emphasized content over form.

To Hicks, William Faulkner had the novelist's power that many writers such as Phillips lacked. But Faulkner, he said, was too preoccupied with sensationalism. His books showed perversity in both form and content; he manipulated point of view and chronology merely for the suspense and shock they created: "What he achieves is not a form rising organically out of the material but an arbitrary pattern." Faulkner's poems showed that he had "a simple heart," and Hicks thought that Faulkner could perhaps develop beyond the sensational, morbid, and psychologically abnormal topics like those of an Edgar Allan Poe or of an Ambrose Bierce. Some episodes in Faulkner's novels showed "a vitality and a kind of veracity that one does not find in the more lurid episodes." His creative facility as a writer might be his greatest danger; he needed to build on the life he understood so well and permit "the organic needs of his material to guide his ingenuity in the creation of new forms." Thus he might get a firmly founded attitude toward life.[23] Hicks showed here several aspects of his criticism at this time: that he was against sensationalism, that he admired imaginative power, that he was interested in the writer's world-attitude, and that, as we have noted, he was a champion of realism. Faulkner's experiments made Hicks impatient; but, like most critics at the time, Hicks did not understand that Faulkner was not strictly a realist.

Some articles that Hicks wrote in 1930 indicate that he was groping for a clearer view of different kinds of novels and of how to classify and evaluate them. He considered Joseph Conrad a philosophical novelist rather than a sociological one like John Galsworthy, Arnold Bennett, or H. G. Wells. Conrad dealt with man's coping in a hostile universe—one in which self-discipline would help a man achieve what there was in life; but, if he failed to succeed against the hostile forces of nature, he still had won an inner victory by adhering to a self-imposed code of conduct. The Conrad kind of novel would always have an appeal for some people, Hicks concluded.[24]

Hicks lamented the trend toward "subjectivity" in the modern fiction such as that of James Joyce, Marcel Proust, Dorothy

Richardson, and Virginia Woolf; he thought the "objective" type such as Hemingway's was more encouraging.[25] The autobiographical novel also held promise, he said, if the writer could detach himself from his characters in the way Thomas Wolfe had been able to do in *Look Homeward, Angel*.[26] And the fiction of Ford Madox Ford seemed a possible answer to the difficulties of both the sociological novel and the experimental novel, either of the Joyce or the John Dos Passos type. Following after Henry James, Ford was writing what might be called the "psychological novel," but he was neglected perhaps because his type of novel was out of style. Ford did demonstrate, however, the vitality of the Jamesian novel. Hicks suggested that, as the experimental novels declined in favor, perhaps Ford's work would receive more attention.[27] Of course, the experimental novel did not really decline, except for the radicals' emphasis on the novel of social protest in the 1930s. And Ford never achieved great attention. Indeed, Hicks later decided that Ford was not so good as he had thought.

V   *Summing Up the Early Years*

We can see in summary, then, that Hicks had established several social and critical principles in his early years as a critic; and he retained many of them when he embraced communism in 1932. His basic philosophical ideas in his pre-Marxist years were the following: (1) that ethics and values were important in literature and that standards for judging literature on this basis should be sought; (2) that the churches were not contributing to the improvement of society; (3) that writers who expressed an affirmation of life and hope for society, if they found firm bases for their ideas, were more valuable than cynical writers; (4) that society needed great writers and critics who could give it unified views of modern life; (5) that the New Humanists like More and Babbitt were too exclusive, dogmatic, and rigid to offer much help; (6) that social involvement was more important than escaping or turning away from society; (7) that, in order for literature to flourish, a better social order had to be established; and (8) that freedom was important and discipline best when self-imposed for rationally held reasons.

Furthermore, we have seen that Hicks explored the problem of the relationship between a just political order, the attitudes of the masses, and the cultured minority. At first he felt that culture for the masses was not as important as a nonexclusive intelligent minority from which the masses could draw culture if they wanted it. Later, he came to believe that a just political solution to basic human needs for the masses took priority over culture for the few. But he did not during this early liberal period suggest that art and literature should be directed to the masses as he was to do when he became a Marxist and urged the development of a proletarian literature.

In speaking specifically of literary works, we have seen that Hicks emphasized the ethical content in most of what he wrote, but he also asserted a few formalist values: the need for fresh words and figures, well-realized and dramatized characters, and dramatic presentation rather than rhetorical discussion of ideas. He concerned himself with classifying novels by using such terms as "experimental," "sociological," and "psychological." In essence, the main thrust and concern of Hicks in his writing was with literature as a reflection of society. He argued that the trouble with modern literature could be traced to the general malaise: American literature reflected a sick society with many false values.

Since the tremendous changes brought about by machines had made the task of the modern artist very difficult, it would take great writers with imaginative power to overcome the obstacles. To Hicks, writers needed some clear vision, some unifying point of view from which to see life and write about it, but he did not spell out what this point of view would be. This was the Granville Hicks who began in the summer of 1931 to reveal an interest in communism as a solution to these problems of a world view. The year 1932 would see the transition completed. We can see in retrospect that his moral earnestness was one cause for his sojourn into such an inflexible, dogmatic school of thought.

CHAPTER 3

Conversion to Communism

MOST liberal intellectuals had been convinced by the end of 1931 that capitalism was doomed, and Hicks was one of them. He began taking steps toward communism during 1931 although he did not actually join the American Communist party until three years later. As a result of his interest in Marxism, he began in 1932 to write in a radical vein, and continued to do so until August, 1939. Since he became a leading spokesman of American Marxist literary criticism, he was an important participant in the literary history of the 1930s.

Hicks had not had much experience with laborers, and he was not suffering from the economic collapse, but he was naturally aware of the severe economic hardships many Americans were experiencing. He concluded that something had to be done; the answer seemed to be to convert America—peacefully—to communism. When Hicks explained in his essays and later in his autobiographical books about how he came to this conclusion, he also delineated how he discovered in Marxist writings the answers to literary questions that had been bothering him. Since he had already suggested that writers needed to deal with industrialism, Marxist criticism seemed to be a literary method that could solve this problem. The battle for change would not be won in the arena of literary criticism, to be sure; but criticism, he felt, would have some significance. He declared that criticism must be a "weapon" if it was not to be "merely an amusing game."[1]

I His Views on Society

During this period 1932–1939, Hicks maintained as part of his social philosophy the basic position that capitalism had to be destroyed, that a nonviolent revolution had to be promoted, and that communism had to be established in America. In his reviews of books on the subject, Hicks argued for and supported the arguments given in defense of communism. Violence might well come, but it would be initiated by desperate capitalists rather than by the workers. Moreover, the capitalists would try to destroy anything that threatened their power over society.[2] As for misgivings about a lack of individual freedom under communism, Hicks reasoned that the disinterestedness and the freedom enjoyed by the elite, such as that which Joseph Wood Krutch claimed we had in a democracy in contrast with communism, had probably never existed anyway, certainly not for most people. The Communists liked accuracy and effectiveness, not amiable detachment. Under the dictatorship of the proletariat, Krutch would have less freedom; but other people would have more, and for the first time. The awareness of individuality would diminish in a collective society, but the opportunities for realizing individual potentialities would increase greatly. And at last in a classless society, Hicks said, minds would be freed from the pull of economic interests.[3]

Other solutions offered to reform society had not and would not work, he argued in the reviews he wrote. Although the utopian communes of the nineteenth century, for example, had been admirable experiments, capitalism had done more good for social improvement. The utopians, however, had kept the ideals alive, while capitalism, he said, had not been able to fulfill the ideals of the bourgeois revolution. The utopians had been impractical, but now a proletarian revolution would carry out their goals.[4] To Hicks, the individual self-improvement that Aldous Huxley advocated would not work better than revolution, for converting individual hearts had been tried for many centuries and had not succeeded. Furthermore, if communism rested on hatred, as Huxley suggested in *Eyeless in Gaza*, it was at its worst a harnessing of hatred toward constructive ends. Historical conditions changed and shaped man; communism taught man how to use this history to cooperate with social forces and thereby shape his destiny.[5] Sinclair Lewis had showed in *It Can't Happen Here* that social responsibility was necessary, but to Hicks something more than protest was needed to save society, and individualistic rebellion such as Lewis's was not enough.[6]

While advocating a Communist revolution as part of his own social philosophy, Hicks, who also spoke out against fascism, thought that Lewis's *It Can't Happen Here* was an effective warning against fascism. This novel could convince the middle class in America of the dangers of fascism and of its demagogues who rose to power on the strength of their radical promises. But Lewis did not show that fascism had a capitalist basis, for Lewis had "not quite freed himself from the notion that fascism is directly caused by the gullibility of the masses and the knavishness and sadism of its leaders." The novel did not point out, he said, that Wall Street wanted to crush the militant members of the working class, nor that there were international reverberations of fascism in America. The book merely advocated that good men be kept in office.[7]

Fascism was also a threat to culture and education, Hicks said in an essay called "The Menace to Culture." With bourgeois culture declining with the decline of capitalism (i.e., the Depression), the menace to culture was evident in the cutbacks of school money, in the suppression of dissent, in the heresy hunts, in the requiring of loyalty oaths from teachers. Capitalists always stultified education to protect their interests, and they would be quite willing to sacrifice American youth rather than surrender their profits. The bourgeois cultural heritage could be preserved and extended only by a (Marxian) socialist society, since capitalism in its decline could become only more barbarous in the form of fascism. Thus Hicks attributed many evils to capitalism and pointed to the manifestations of its death as being the rise of fascism.[8] He later discarded the notion, however, that fascism was necessarily tied to or grew out of capitalism.

Hicks also expressed an impatience with liberalism. However, he could also give qualified praise to such a liberal as E. M. Forster because Forster hated fascism more than he disapproved or distrusted communism. Lincoln Steffens had pointed out, Hicks said, that communism was the party of the poets. Liberalism alone led to no action and could lead to "empty glorification of one's personal preference, i.e., one's more or less unconscious class prejudices." But, when the qualities of passion for life and awareness of human potentialities were combined, the result was a propulsion toward revolution; and Forster had these qualities. Hicks shows in these remarks the Marxist practice of examining a writer's class alliance as an approach to analysis. He also asserts, however, the Communist view that a liberal attitude can lead to inaction.[9]

Another characteristic of Hicks's social philosophy during this period was his belief in the industrial way of life and his rejection of antiindustrial ideas; and he carried this idea from his pre-Marxist years. Since the belief in the industrial way of life—under the control of the proletariat and socialized, of course—is a major element of Communist ideology, Hicks felt comfortable with it after becoming a Marxist. As we saw in the previous chapter, he had already taken this position in his 1929 essay "Industry and the Imagination," and in 1937 Hicks criticized Ford Madox Ford (whom he had praised in 1930) because of Ford's retreat from industry. Ford, who had become aware of the evils of war, imperialism, and economic injustice, proposed to abolish these evils by encouraging small producers and by doing away with mass production—and all was to be brought about by a general change of heart, which, in turn, was to be accomplished by the arts. This small-producer program, Hicks asserted, was futile; for mass production of food enabled more people to have a variety diet that was better than home production could ever achieve. Hicks concluded that Ford did not have an "intellectual center" and did not know where he was going.[10]

In 1938 Hicks published his friendly, folksy book *I Like America* that advocated communism. He asserted that Americans could work together collectively to establish socialism in order to eliminate poverty and to provide plenty. This step was, he argued, the next logical one in the history of America; and his book made taking the step seem very easy and sensible. But Hicks, who had had only limited experience with industrial work, ignored many of the hard realities of it. He said nothing of the stultifying work in a factory, nor of the problem of how to humanize industry. He simply assumed that socialism would make all work and all conditions better.[11]

During this period of the United Front, Hicks and other Communists wrote in a conciliatory manner. Replying to letters from readers of his book *I Like America*, Hicks said in *New Masses* that citizens should support labor unions, protect free speech, oppose fascism, and work for government policies that united peaceful nations against fascist nations. If capitalism declined, then people would see that "the only way to protect the American standard of living is for the people to take over the means of production. In other words, we believe that these very measures will lead to the establishment of socialism, which is our goal. If we are wrong, if abundance for all is compatible with the continuance of the Capitalist system, then you win. In fact, as I see it, you win either way."[12] Hicks remained consistent in his social ideas during his Marxist period, but he felt more comfortable with the soft line of the United Front years of the second half of the decade than with the earlier hard line. His friendly approach and his faith in sweet reason did not account for the raw, naked power that Stalin was using in Russia. What Hicks had heard about that power, he suppressed within himself—until the Stalin-Hitler pact.

II *Literature and Reform*

To Hicks, literature and literary criticism were to play a part in the social revolution; and he expressed four basic ideas concerning the relationship between literature and society. One was that the most important literature was that which dealt with central issues, and the central issue was the class struggle. The second idea was that the writer who interpreted society clearly would express the attitude of the militant proletarians and would convey a mood of hope rather than one of futility and pessimism. The third was that critics and writers on the left had to develop and promote proletarian literature. The fourth and last was that the great literature of America had always been in the "great tradition" of rebellion and criticism of the ills of society.

In arguing that important writers dealt with the great issues of their times, Hicks gave a special Marxist slant to an idea he had already expressed. The central issue of his time became not just coping with industry but with the decline of capitalism and with the struggle of the workers to win freedom. A sensitive writer felt the pressure of his age exerted upon him, Hicks reasoned. No writer was free; he could run away, but only by paying a price. A great writer was not damaged by the pressure his age put upon him, although minor writers often crumbled. Hicks recommended that American writers do what the Russian novelist Sholokhov had done in *Seeds of Tomorrow*. In order to tell the story of collectivization in Russia, Sholokhov had so immersed himself in the life he was describing that his book had the accuracy of expert diagnosis along with a living, realistic story. Sholokhov's great talent had flourished, he said, under the pressures of his age.[13]

Great writers could not abandon the struggle, Hicks asserted in a paper delivered at the Second Writer's Congress in 1937; for their escape would only lead to more frustration. Where in the confusion of America were "the generous impulses . . . the seeing eye and the feeling heart?" They were in the radical writers. But what should writers do to fight war and fascism since they could not remain aloof? Certainly, they had to do their writing; and, by their writing and by other means, they had to "make the world a place in which good writing can be done." Although some writers allowed organizations to absorb them, "No writer can afford to let a party or a union do his thinking for him. He may properly act in unison with his group, but the only kind of thinking fit for his books is his own. We have an advantage over earlier writers because we have a sense of belonging to America," he told his audience at the congress. "In the masses who are marching with us we have companions and we have a potential, if not actual, audience." Some of the writers present at the Writer's Congress would do great work in the coming years, Hicks said, and their books would "march in step with the marching feet of millions, and they will be as great as the tasks of these coming years are great."[14] Hicks had a vision of the future that would be made possible by writers who confronted the issues and "marched" with the workers who were soon to assert themselves—inevitably.

Many writer did not satisfy Hicks, and in his reviews in the *New Masses* he condemned them for their failures. But some succeeded, he thought. To be sure, even the writers whom he praised never quite lived up to his full expectations of the ideal revolutionary writer; but at least they were working toward that goal and were not being evasive like the "bourgeois" writers. Hicks had the most praise for John Dos Passos, especially for *1919* and *The 42nd Parallel* (the first two volumes of the trilogy *U.S.A.*). Robert Cantwell in *The Land of Plenty* had done well, although he had not shown in the end of the novel the "unconquerable militance of the workers," and he had "failed to sweep the reader along." Hicks liked, with qualifications, Grace Lumpkin's novels *A Sign for Cain* and *To Make My Bread*. He said Fielding Burke's first novel *A Stone Came Rolling* made the labor struggle central to the story and was thus better than her second novel, *Call Home the Heart*. B. Tavern had the proletarian insight in *The Treasure of the Sierra Madre*; and Ralph Bates (British) had done well, Hicks said, in *Lean, The Olive Field*, and *Rainbow Fish*. The virtues of these radical novels grew out of the writers' revolutionary convictions. For example, Albert Halper in *The Foundry* and *The Chute* had given insight into workers and their environment; for he showed that they were made of "good human stuff, the stuff out of which rebellion can and will be made." Hicks also had praise for Richard Wright's collection of stories *Uncle Tom's Children*. And at last in 1939 came John Steinbeck's *The Grapes of Wrath*, which did almost everything the ideal revolutionary novel was to do.[15]

The radical novelists were not perfect, but they showed more vitality than the aesthetes, the regionalists, the pessimists, or the romantics, Hicks argued.[16] A good many writers were dodging the central issues; and among these authors in the 1930s was Ernest Hemingway, because of *Death in the Afternoon* and *Green Hills of Africa* and because of his turning away from the subjects he had written about in the 1920s. (In 1937 when Hemingway published *To Have and Have Not*, Hicks praised the novel, as we will see in chapter 4.)[17] Willa Cather, too, was turning from current issues and was seeking to escape into the romantic past of the frontier. Thomas Mann in Europe was also indulging in evasion, for *Joseph and His Brothers* was merely an entertaining interpretation of the biblical story. Bourgeois writers tried to rely on sensibility and personal experience, Hicks said, to escape the issues. Although Proust and Joyce had presented accurate pictures, their imitators did not; and in this category were Elizabeth Madox Roberts, Thomas Wolfe, William Faulkner, and Virginia Woolf.[18]

Since the class struggle and the coming revolution were the important subjects of literature to the Hicks of this period, the novels that best fulfilled this purpose were those that showed hope and militant zeal in the workers as opposed to those novels which expressed frustration, pessimism, or docility. Hicks thought that many novels about workers were unsatisfactory because they failed to show the existence of this militancy among at least some workers. Frank Tilsley's *The Plebian's Progress*, he said, was one that failed in this way; for, although it at least made people think, it did not make them want to act. Since pessimism was harmful in a proletarian novel, Hicks did not like Andre Malraux's *Man's Fate*. Malraux was, however, still valuable; for he had insight into the mental processes of the masses; and, "though he does not portray their role correctly, he does magnificently convey their emotions." Walter Greenwood's *Love on the Dole* was a good English proletarian novel, but it was not sufficiently revolutionary. His second novel, *The Time Is Ripe*, was good, however, because it "made the reader conscious on every page of the enormous latent capacities of the proletariat."[19]

In 1937 Hicks answered those who wrote to the *New Masses* to criticize his insistence upon hope and militancy. In his reply, Hicks asserted that communism was "good news" that gave writers a sense of affirmation and clarity. He had been insisting on these ideas and attitudes in radical novels because he felt they should convey this hopefulness. He admitted that writers might have sometimes substituted slogans for reality and stereotyped situations for concrete experience. He had sometimes tolerated "the formula of the conversion story or the formula of the strike novel . . . because I know there is a dramatic reality in conversion and a powerful story in a strike." Many writers of this generation had grown up reading the writers of despair, he argued, and these writers had always expressed conviction. The ones who tried to show hope deserved to be encouraged.[20]

When Muriel Rukeyser challenged Hicks on the problem of hope in a symposium reply in *New Masses*, she insisted that the rigid standard of the happy ending was useless and that it had proved to be so every time it had been applied to left-wing literature. "A good many people feel now that whatever excellence the left-wing writers have depends more on their sensitive straight facing of present scenes and values than on the happy posturing of their theses." Hope in such books was not "the familiar one but another, profounder one, by which writers can touch their time and their country and not find the sweetness and light here called for, but its life and a steadier, less blatant hope than Mr. Hicks demands—a hope to be worked for continually, not shouted before its time."[21] When Hicks tried to answer Rukeyser, he was unable to counter her argument effectively. Indeed, Hicks's idea that a leftist novel should show militant hopefulness was one of his less fortunate theories.

Concurrent with the theory of revolutionary hope was the idea that Marxists had to encourage, promote, and single out as good writing the fiction that was about the masses; and Hicks undertook to do so. Literature was to be used as a class weapon, as a way of creating sympathy and brotherhood among the masses. There was talk about "proletarian literature" that was defined as both that *about* the proletariat (even if by bourgeois writers) and *by* members of the proletariat. Hicks talked also of "collective novels" that had a group rather than a person as their hero.[22]

During the year 1934, as literary editor of the *New Masses*, Hicks wrote a great deal about the problem of writing and about getting a readership for the proletarian novel. And he continued to praise and call attention to proletarian works, while also attacking such romantic, middle-class novels as the best-seller *Anthony Adverse* by Hervey Allen, as well as works by Thornton Wilder, Pearl Buck, and Lloyd Douglas.[23]

After becoming literary editor, Hicks wrote a series for *New Masses* that was entitled "Revolution and the Novel."[24] Presented in seven installments, it was a kind of creative writing course and catechism for revolutionary writers. In this series, Hicks set forth his ideas about (1) the selection of form for a novel, (2) the use of the past and future in novels, (3) drama and biography as models, (4) characterization, (5) selection and emphasis, (6) documentation, and (7) the future of proletarian fiction. Besides his reviewing and a few other essays, this series represented Hicks's most extensive effort to foster proletarian literature.

Some of his discussions were so elementary as to be almost insulting to an intelligent writer with any experience at all, while other parts were extremely didactic and dogmatic. For example, in dealing with the selection of characters to write about, part 4 divided them into classes. Among the working class, Hicks said, the writer had to choose among those who were already class conscious, those who became so during the novel, and those who did not so awaken. To Hicks, no American had written of the workers who were already class conscious, but Michael Gold and Jack Conroy had portrayed the workers who had developed such sensitivity. Writing about the workers who did not become class conscious was the most difficult because it was hard to deal with and overcome hopelessness, Hicks warned; and Edward Dahlberg and Erskine Caldwell had this weakness of expressing no hope. The revolutionary writer did not feel hopeless and did not want to convey this attitude to his readers, "and yet he knows that slogans and sermons will not serve his purpose, and he will not resort to falsification." Hicks added, however, that novels like those by Dahlberg, Caldwell, and James T. Farrell served a purpose because they analyzed sectors of American life and indicted the capitalist system. Hicks also talked of the opportunities and dangers of writing about middle-class characters, about farmers, about the trials of artists among Philistines, about the leftward movement of intellectuals, and about the bourgeois fellow traveler.

The first six parts of the series were an attempt to establish a formula for revolutionary fiction. Despite his qualifying remarks that formulas were no substitute for imagination and that writing must not be mechanical, Hicks not only was prescribing ways of writing proletarian novels but also was seeking a surefire way to have writers express the truth from the Marxian point of view. Since he believed very strongly that Marxism was the truth, his advocacy is not any more surprising than an agent's suggesting to a pulp-fiction writer a formula for being entertaining and salable. But the possibilities of a lack of spontaneity and creativity in the writer are obvious.

In part 7, Hicks asserted that proletarian literature, even when it was faulty, was important and that its role in bringing about revolution might be decisive. Revolutionary authors often seemed clumsy, he said, because they were trying to express a new type of sensibility. And radicals responded to such work, in spite of its faults, because they were moving in the same direction. No revolutionary novelist had done what Marcel Proust had done for bourgeois life, not even Dos Passos, Hicks said. A proletarian masterpiece would "do justice to all the many-sided richness of its characters, exploring with Proustian persistence the deepest recesses of individuality and at the same time exhibiting that individuality as essentially a social phenomenon." Although such a novel might not appear for a while, the growth of proletarian literature showed the power of the movement. It was, Hicks said, "indispensable . . . for intensifying and organizing the vague impulses toward rebellion that are the foundation of the revolutionary state of mind." Thus, to Hicks, literature was very important to society, and proletarian literature would help create the society he was sure was coming.

Hicks had argued even early in his career, as we noted, that the most important literature in America had always been concerned with society and its ills. This concern was the "great tradition" in American literature—the tradition of realism, rebellion, and criticism. Although Hicks maintained this thesis throughout his Marxist years, he expressed it most completely, of course, in *The Great Tradition* which was first published in 1933 and which was reissued in a revised edition in 1935 that contained a section about more recent revolutionary novels. To Hicks, the earlier American writers had lacked the clarifying vision and the insights that Marxism provided. Since communism was the logical heir to their critical and rebellious tradition, the frustration of earlier American writers could now disappear. In summing up his book, Hicks reiterated this idea:

This is the great tradition of American literature. Ours has been a critical literature, critical of greed, cowardice, and meanness. It has been a hopeful literature, touched again and again with a passion for brotherhood, justice, and intellectual honesty. That the writers of the past could not have conceived of the revolutionary literature of today and would, perhaps, repudiate it if they were alive, makes no difference. We see that the fulfillment of their ideals involves far more than they realized. It involves not merely fulfilling but also transcending their vision. It involves not merely criticism but destruction of capitalism and its whole way of life. But the alternative is fascism's sadistic extinction of every noble hope the past has fostered.[25]

The book expresses his main ideas on the relationship between society and literature. Since it is his first major attempt at an analysis of literature from a Marxist point of view, it is discussed more extensively in chapter 4.

Hicks made another effort at striking a blow for revolution through literature, as we mentioned in chapter 1, with his biography of John Reed, the American journalist who was present for the Bolshevik Revolution and who wrote *Ten Days That Shook the World* (1919). A Harvard graduate, Reed had fallen in love with Pancho Villa's revolution in Mexico and written about it; he had subsequently returned home to write about labor struggles and to protest in general about social injustice. After that, he had gone to Russia in time for the Revolution, had become a Communist, and had died in Russia of typhus during his second trip there.

Since John Reed Clubs had been formed in the United States by the American Communist party, it was logical that they would want a biography of Reed. Hicks was chosen to write one, along with John Stuart, who became Hicks's research assistant. Although this biography is very readable and seems accurate, a controversy later developed about whether Reed had become disillusioned with communism just before he died. Hicks was later accused of withholding such facts, but he effectively refuted the accusation.[26]

III *Shortcomings of His Views*

Because of his views about capitalism and about literature's proper role in society, we have seen that Hicks concluded that he must work for communism and for revolutionary literature. In retrospect, it seems clear that his assumptions were faulty ones for several reasons. Hicks and most other radicals did not foresee the resiliency of capitalism because of government fiscal manipulation and welfare programs. He suggested that the choice lay between communism and fascism, when in fact no such choice was necessary: a middle way was found which, at least for the next few decades, seemed to work. Whether capitalism will eventually be supplanted by socialism (or something else) remains to be seen, but any such change will no doubt come about more slowly than Hicks expected. We could also argue, of course, that the threat of radicalism forced the government to modify its policies. At any rate, when prosperity returned, the fires of revolution were dampened.

Ironically, Hicks saw the role of the revolutionary critic much as a church minister might see his role in judging interpretations of church dogma and in pointing out heresies. To Hicks, literary critics were the high priests of Marxist culture. As such, Hicks's own most glaring critical error was in insisting that proletarian literature should express militancy and hope, for writers could not superimpose hopefulness upon their work if they did not feel it. Presenting life as they saw it in all its complexity was the only way to express it, as Hicks later admitted: "What all of us might have realized was that the young writers were wiser in the doubts that crept into their work than they were in their political affirmations."[27]

Whether revolutionary literature represented the culmination of the "great tradition" in America was and is a matter of opinion. Insofar as revolutionary literature represented a continuation of the humanistic tradition and was the work of persons who disapproved of injustice, ugliness, and meanness, it was a worthy part of the tradition. But whether the American literature, past and present, that dealt with specific social ills represented the only great literature remained a matter of taste and personal choice. Although it was time for more writers to turn to America and its people for subject matter, and although some writers needed to deal with social problems, Hicks expected too much from literature as a revolutionary weapon.

His series of articles on how to write revolutionary novels, while presenting many good ideas about the problems and the types of fiction, did not contain the kind of instruction that would improve literature, whether revolutionary or nonrevolutionary. Especially bad were the parts in which he tried to prescribe not only the proper subjects to write about but also the ideas the writer was to express. Creative genius will manage either to survive such exhortation and prevail in spite of it, or it will slip away from it altogether and find its own path to human truth. The critic does have a social function, and in many ways Hicks contributed to the critical process, but the critic's role is somewhat less direct and programmatic than Hicks conceived it to be.

CHAPTER 4

Marxist Method and Practice

I   *His Critical Principles*

AS we have noted in chapter 3, Hicks conceived the radical critic's role to be a useful part of the revolution. While fulfilling the public role of the critic, he wrote several essays outlining his proposed application of Marxism to literature. Meanwhile, he applied his theory in his book reviews and in his two books of criticism, *The Great Tradition* and *Figures of Transition*, and he also retained some of the critical ideas he had expounded in his pre-Marxist days.

When Hicks began to assert the values of this Marxist criticism in 1932, one of his basic assertions was that the class struggle was the fundamental fact of life and was thus the basic approach to analysis. In "Literary Criticism and the Marxian Method" (1932), he said that the writer had to understand the conflict of the classes to get at the basis of a situation. The most important writers dealt with the central issues of the time, and the class struggle was that issue in this age. Although a writer could use the past as a subject, he had to handle those aspects of it that had some relevance for his own time. For example, Michael Gold had been right, Hicks said, in asserting that Thornton Wilder's novels were unrelated to modern Americans' lives, that his characters were unconvincing, and that his style was pretentious and imitative. As a result, Hicks charged that Wilder displayed no artistic integrity and that he was pandering to a pseudoaristocracy.

A good Marxist critic, to Hicks, did not use his philosophy in a narrow way. Although he did regard the status of the forces of industrial production at the time of a literary work, he did not apply this information directly. Because such a Marxist writer looked at the social situation and at the ideas that develop as a "superstructure" upon the basis of the productive methods, his method was more inclusive than that of others, such as academic examinations of intellectual influences. The Marxists knew that these socioeconomic forces influenced a writer's views, but they did so according to the class from which he came: "They believe that the person who looks at life from the point of view of the exploiting class inevitably distorts it, whereas the person who regards it from the proletarian point of view is capable of accurate and clarifying interpretation." The Marxists knew also that upper-class writers could be good, although fragmentary, and that proletarians could be poor writers. They used Marx "as a compass rather than a yardstick."

Hicks concluded the essay by arguing that the built-in conflict between the proletarian class and the exploiting capitalist class resulted from their relationship with each other in handling the forces of production. Thus, the class struggle and the importance of the forces of basic economic activity revealed much about everything, even literature. Writers would profit, Hicks said, by viewing their world from the position of the proletariat—a position that gives them a clarifying and energizing insight. And literature, if it were to help shape the revolution, had to be used as a weapon.[1]

Hicks soon got his opportunity to contribute to the battle; for, in "An Open Letter" in 1934 to prospective reviewers for the *New Masses*, he stated his hopes about what the leftist critics could accomplish. Reviewers would have freedom to express diverse views and to apply their Marxist principles in their own ways. Although they had to be well informed to combat criticism from opponents, they were not to be bookish or pedantic. Their task was to "interpret the intellectual currents and the emotional forces of our time as they are reflected in literature." The literary battle gave the critics their chance to contribute to the revolution, he said, and it was with this opportunity that they would succeed or fail.[2]

When Hicks attempted to clarify the problems facing Marxist critics and to suggest a critical procedure in his article "The Crisis in American Criticism" (1933), he asserted that Marxism offered the only clear method of explanation and evaluation of literature. To Hicks, V. F. Calverton's earlier attempt, *The Liberation of American Literature*, had been too abstract and had reduced aesthetic categories to economic ones. This fault could be avoided by concentrating on the individual writer and his work, for the fundamental dependence of literature on the economic organization of society could still be shown. After the writer's attitude toward life had been defined by examining the relevant biography, history, and psychology, the expression of that attitude in his works could be considered. After defining the author's attitude toward life, the critic could then "examine the aesthetic forms in which the given attitude can express itself when concerned with the given material." Technical criticism could also be used, but the basic questions about economic relations would have been answered first. This approach would bridge the gap between "the analysis of the author's class status and the analysis of his finished literary product" (which is what Calverton had failed to do).

Continuing, Hicks said that evaluation was more difficult. The primary assumption was, to Hicks, that literature was to be judged by its *effects* on its readers. It was an error, however, to expect a book to make a reader go out and do a specific thing. The aim of the creative writer was to present life as he saw it. The work would thus affect the reader's attitude toward life. Not all readers would react alike, but not all responses were purely personal. As a rule, certain groups responded in certain ways, and the class alignment of a person was the most important factor. Since the role of the proletarian was historically important, the critic was justified in considering the effect of literature on the proletariat rather than on any other class; but no statistical evidence of the final effects could be secured. The critic had to proceed "by studying the possible effect of a piece of literature on the attitudes of persons performing the proletarian role." In this respect, Hicks led himself into one of the pitfalls of his philosophy; for, by reasoning that the critic had to consider the effect of a work on a proletarian, he reached the position described in chapter 3 of insisting that proletarian novels express militancy and revolutionary hope.

Although the critic would insist that the literary work be concerned with central issues of life, a novel would have to so describe the effects of the class struggle that the reader would feel that he was participating in the lives of the characters. This sense was to come, not from technique, but from the author's understanding of experience, which in turn, Hicks asserted, was related to his attitude toward life. The author's view should be that of the "vanguard of the proletariat," and he had to make as complete an identification with the proletariat as possible. This kind of literature would arouse a sense of solidarity among the workers by creating "an attitude . . . capable of extension and adaptation to any situation." It would, for example, force the reader to recognize the complete unworthiness of the existing system and would also arouse in him the hope and power of the working class. It would give him a view of reality that would "galvanize him into action" on behalf of the proletariat.

Hicks came very close to contradicting himself in this essay when he stated that the reader would adopt an attitude but would not be moved to do one specific thing and then later asserted that the reader would be "galvanized into action." Clearly, Hicks saw the purpose of literature (at least of the revolutionary kind) as fairly direct in its effect, in spite of his attempt to qualify his statements. Literature was not to be only for enjoyment, insight, expanding of experience, while the politics was left to the party and to the labor movement. Literature was to have a more direct role—it was to promote action; and Hicks saw the critic, in effect, as playing the role of recruiter of writers for the revolutionary cause.[3] Although the Marxists did not need to convert non-Marxist critics but did have to meet their arguments, the Marxists needed to reach the young writers and bring them to the Marxist side. Marxists had to clarify their position and improve their practice and work together.

In summary, Hicks's theories based on Marxism encompassed the centrality of the class struggle, the importance of the forces of economic production, the use of literature as a weapon, the value of knowing the writer's class alliance and his attitudes, and the evaluation of literature according to its effects upon the proletarian reader.

II   *Two Non-Marxist Principles*

During this period Hicks expressed two other ideas that are related to—but not directly tied with—his Marxist theories. The first non-Marxist idea was that form and content were inseparable; the second was that the assumptions the author expressed in his work were important and should be examined in the analysis and teaching of literature. Although Hicks later dropped the first idea, he retained the second (at least implicitly) during the remainder of his career.

Although Hicks had in his pre-Marxist days asserted this idea that matters of form could not be discussed separately from content, he restated and elaborated upon this view in the 1930s. The failures, for example, of the muckraking novelists at the turn of the century, Hicks argued, came from their failure to find a satisfactory point of view. Although the critic could indicate the authors' stylistic problems, these considerations were secondary and were rooted in the other problem.[4] For another example, Hicks argued that V. F. Calverton, in his book on Marxist criticism, had failed to show the relationship of craftsmanship to content. Technique could be studied alone, but "the creative process is essentially a unit and . . . the more important problems of form are absolutely bound up in the problems of content and attitude." Calverton had accepted this idea, Hicks said, but he had not put it into practice.[5]

Hicks repeated this theory several times during the 1930s, for he felt he had hit upon an important idea. He was never able, however, to show how form and content were indissolubly related or how a work could be thoroughly analyzed and criticized in regard to such unity. What he ended doing was to assert, in essence, that, if the content was bad, good form did not make any difference. As a result, Hicks finally abandoned his content-form concept.

The second idea, the importance of examining assumptions, was expressed in one of his better critical essays during his radical period. In "Assumptions in Literature" (1936), published in the *English Journal*, Hicks argued that a writer reflected his unconscious prejudices and presuppositions in his writing. Although the critic's or the teacher's job was to help readers and students become aware of some of these hidden premises, these professionals might not look either critically or intensively enough at these premises, especially in the works of modern writers, to discover them. Since literature did affect its readers, Hicks argued that it was important to point out possibly harmful or untruthful hidden assumptions. Certainly no one wanted to sponsor or start burning books, he said; but, since writers were emotional people, their prejudices had to be watched for and scrutinized critically.

When Hicks gave several examples, he cited Henry James, who assumed that a small world of leisure-class people represented civilization. Many readers who probably enjoyed an unconscious snob appeal from reading James would profit from a critical look

at this assumption, which Hicks called an "obvious falseness."
Thomas Wolfe would probably deny any prejudice against
Negroes or Jews, but he had let it creep into *Of Time and the
River*. And in all of the discussion and praise of Margaret Mitch-
ell's *Gone With the Wind*, Hicks said, no one had ever thought of
pointing out her assumed attitudes toward Negroes. Another example was the martial attitude toward war expressed in Tennyson's "The Charge of the Light Brigade." And slick fiction sold
the idea of the American dream: that hard work would always
bring wealth and success. After pointing out that the assumptions
were certainly not all there was to analyzing a literary work,
Hicks stated that they were an important part. People wondered
where students got their prejudices, but they often came from influences such as literature, and teachers had to be concerned.[6]

Hicks made a pertinent point here, for he was propounding one
aspect of criticism that has often been neglected. Formalist critics
are so concerned with the examination of a work of art in terms of
its characteristics as a genre that they tend to ignore or to evade
the emotional or ideological issues and do not attempt to extract
the assumptions from a work. Of course, a person might have a
narrow view himself, as the Marxists often did, but their political
position was obvious because it was usually stated openly. Yet
many of the formalists of the 1930s had an aristocratic bias,
which they refused to acknowledge.

III   *Hicks as a Practicing Marxist*

While advocating the Marxist approach to literary analysis,
Hicks also put into practice the methods that he was urging other
critics (and teachers) to adopt in critical reviews and books.
Although his application of critical principles can be seen in the
dozens of book reviews that he wrote during the 1930s, one of his
most illuminating reviews was of Marcel Proust's *A Remem-
brance of Things Past*. Hicks, who had become fascinated with
Proust at the beginning of the decade, confessed to having
become deeply absorbed in reading all of this long novel. By
1934, when he wrote his review, he was not sure that Proust
would be good reading for proletarians. In the coming post-
revolutionary period, Proust might be forgotten, Hicks said; for
Proust did not reveal fundamental truths about humanity. Artists
liked his philosophy because it suggested that the artist's

reconstruction of past experience was the only reality. What Proust gave us of value was a picture of the life of a certain people at a certain time. He showed the decay and ineffectuality of the French aristocracy and the nauseating corruption of the petty-bourgeois social climber. His characters from the lower order of society were shown to be stronger and finer, though they, unfortunately according to Hicks, were not class conscious in the Marxist sense.

Proust, he continued, was partly detached from the aristocracy and was serious about his art: "Detachment from a decadent class is a virtue when it brings freedom from the artifices and illusions with which that class consoles and deceives itself." Although Proust saw much very clearly, he would not be chosen for the future, Hicks said, as a model for Communist writers; his methods of writing were tied to his attitude toward life. Writers could, however, learn to understand a bygone age by reading Proust, and they could get some enjoyment from it, as well as some "moments of acute disgust." Although workers would not benefit by reading him, revolutionary thinkers could profit by doing so in order to understand the decadence of the bourgeois class and to break away from the bourgeoisie themselves. Proust, in a limited way, could help them achieve not only understanding but action.[7]

All the critical approaches to literary criticism that Hicks had outlined for the critic are in operation here, for he had looked at the background and class alignment of Proust. He had examined the implications and assumptions behind Proust's novels, and he had considered the effect the novels might have on their readers. He had noted the way Proust portrayed the lower classes, and he had considered (briefly) the methods that Proust used to convey his world attitude. Proust's class alignment did not completely distort his portrayal of the lower and upper classes, Hicks said, because Proust was partly detached from them.

The treatment of class alignment outlined and practiced by Hicks in this example demonstrates a flaw in his conception. For, if Proust was partly detached from his class, could that not be because he had the integrity of the true artist? Perhaps any artist, even proletarian writers, must be so detached. We do not reject Hicks's idea that the critic needs to consider the artist's background, for his background, including class, should be taken into account. But surely the great artist overcomes, for the most part, this class alliance; and Proust—by Hicks's own admission—seems to do that. Hicks's emphasis on class alignment did not lead him astray on Proust, since he admitted Proust was partly detached; but Hicks sometimes applied his class alignment criterion super-ficially, especially in treating "bourgeois" and "proletarian" writers who were producing during the 1930s.

Hicks again argued that a writer was affected by his class when he reviewed a book about the poet Vachel Lindsay. The values of the middle class made writers from that group suffer, Hicks observed, since that class was morally and intellectually bankrupt. Lindsay's disintegration had been caused by the fact that he was a middle-class poet who never questioned his class values and who had no audience to respond to his work. His ideals, such as agrarianism, were "outdated." He ended in suicide, and his death was a "social tragedy." Since Lindsay had not been able to grow, Hicks concluded, he had de-teriorated—and died.[8]

Probably more factors were involved in Lindsay's death than his class alignment. An inadequate sense of values or a lack of social insights may have been part of his troubles, but attributing these to the American middle class in the rigid fashion that Hicks did seems narrow and inflexible. The upper and lower classes held many values that were hardly different from those of the middle class. Analyzing a writer like Lindsay, with no documen-tation of the cause-effect connections, produces dubious results. Hicks did say important things in such reviews—not about class alignments, but about the values and assumptions held in our society and reflected by writers.

In dealing with novels published in the 1930s, Hicks was impa-tient with those that did not treat social problems; and he also tended to place too high a value on books that did. For example, his preoccupation with social involvement led him astray when he reviewed Ernest Hemingway's *To Have and Have Not* in 1937. Earlier he had castigated Hemingway for seeking escape in drink-ing, bull fights, violence (including big game hunting), and sex. Hicks was so overjoyed when this later novel appeared that he argued that Harry Morgan was Hemingway's "most completely realized character"—better than Jake Barnes in *The Sun Also Rises* and Frederick Henry in *A Farewell to Arms*. To Hicks, Hemingway portrayed the contemptible "haves" with "a kind of quiet fury that I have never felt in his work before." These "haves" included the idle rich, yacht owners, a drunken professor, and a pseudoproletarian novelist.

As for Harry Morgan, we could all admire him as Hemingway did, Hicks said, "but we can see that his way of individual lawless violence, however heroic in itself, could not work. The remarkable thing . . . is that Hemingway sees it too." Morgan was different from his other characters because he was "firmly rooted in a real world," and Hemingway could see that no "have-not" alone could defeat the "haves." It was his best novel, Hicks said, because of Hemingway's "increasing awareness of the character of the economic system and the social order it dominates."[9]

Hicks was wrong about the novel; for, although Hemingway had tried to show contempt for the "haves," he had not portrayed them with any force. Actually, that section is the weakest part of Hemingway's novel. Morgan was a well-realized character, but his portrayal is no better than that of Hemingway's other characters. Hemingway also makes it plain in the novel that he had no use either for proletarian novels or for revolution; for he shows Morgan's contempt for the Cuban revolutionaries.

Furthermore, the novel does not necessarily show that rebellious individualism is not so good as collectivism. Although Morgan does say, as he lies dying, that no man alone has a chance, his comment can as easily be taken for a lament about the passing of rugged individualism as for a conversion to collectivism. Moreover, nothing Morgan does as a character leads the reader to believe that he has much faith in collective action by workers, since he has as much contempt for the average worker's ability to fight for himself—although he is sympathetic—as he does for most radicals. Although Hemingway is not against democratic ideals and humane treatment of common people, he does not express much hope for their improvement.

The truth is that the novel is confused; it has good passages but lacks overall unity. The narrative point of view shifts confusingly. Hemingway seems to be saying that vital, brave people like Harry Morgan are surrounded by weak, mean people from all classes. The effect is closer to sophomoric cynicism than high tragedy, and certainly the novel has no kinship with revolutionary or melioristic fiction. Hicks should have seen that Hemingway was not a radical novelist.

IV   The Great Tradition

Many other examples could be given of Hicks as a critical reviewer, but his comments about the above-mentioned writers will serve to illustrate his Marxist approach. As has been observed, Hicks first applied his Marxist analysis on a large scale in *The Great Tradition* (1933)[10] in which he interpreted American literature published after the Civil War. Throughout the book, Hicks concerned himself with the classes which the authors wrote about, with their personal backgrounds, with the political views of both the authors and their fictional characters, and with the writers' frustrations and lack of full development, which he related to their failure to grasp the necessity for social revolution. Although Hicks discussed many writers and presented many summary evaluations and comments about the authors, his main focus was on economics and politics. Hicks was concerned with the decline of the agrarian, mercantile ways and with the rise of capitalistic industry as the economic causes of the American writers' attitudes and frustrations.

Dealing first in the book with the writers who had developed before 1865, Hicks observed that the end of the Civil War had meant the beginning of capitalistic industry as the dominant economic force. Ralph Waldo Emerson, Henry David Thoreau, Nathaniel Hawthorne, and Herman Melville, in spite of their achievements, did not have much to say to the postwar generations, Hicks asserted, because they did not deal with industrialism and the people who had to live with it. James Russell Lowell, who had primarily identified with the tradition of respectability, had only late in his career taken up the abolitionist cause; and, in his old age, he had fostered European literature. Walt Whitman had expressed the democratic impulse of the masses, but he had not considered how the forces would be controlled to bring about the society he dreamed of.

The regionalist literary movement had offered some promise in Bret Harte, Mark Twain, Edward Eggleston, George Washington Cable, Sarah Orne Jewett, and others, Hicks said, but regional cultures had not been allowed to flourish before they were disintegrated by the forces of industrialism. Harte had turned out to be a mere entertainer who used the devices of the local color writers. Mark Twain had failed to grasp the importance of his writing about the frontier and had not had the power to see the hidden relations among the men and events he knew so well. He was the prime example, Hicks said, of the American writer whose potential had not been realized because of his lack of a revolutionary vision. Eggleston and Cable tried to capture the character of their regions; but, since they had looked backward for the most part and had indulged in nostalgia, they had evaded present realities.

Writers who had tried to deal with the realities of the Gilded Age had done better, Hicks said, but they too had failed to find a unifying theme, even though they had showed the corruption and the demoralization of the nation. Among these were Charles Dudley Warner in his novel *The Gilded Age* (written with Mark Twain), Henry Adams in *Democracy*, and William Dean Howells, especially in his novel *The Rise of Silas Lapham*, in which Lapham decides not to sacrifice his integrity for his business and ends in poverty. The Howells novel suggested there was corruption and temptation in the business world, Hicks said, and this suggestion was too bold for much of the reading public, even though most captains of industry had not suffered from such scruples as Lapham had. Only Howells had persistently tried, Hicks said, to write of his own era, but he was limited and confused and therefore superficial; however, Howells had pushed literature in the right direction of realism.

Henry James, Emily Dickinson, and Sarah Orne Jewett had gotten some good results in their flight from the difficult realities and complexities of their time in America. Jewett portrayed in her stories the old virtues of the Maine village life that she had known; she aroused a similar response in the reader; but she was limited, Hicks argued, by an elegiac subject matter. James had made contributions in his experiments with narrative point of view in fiction but had been limited because he saw the artist as an observer rather than as a participant in life. His contacts with the social realities, Hicks suggested, were too fragmentary and tenuous for him to have more than secondary value to the majority of readers. Dickinson gained power by cutting herself off from her vulgar age and by writing with integrity, yet her poetry, Hicks concluded, was fragile and remote and did not express the society of which she was a part.

Writers of the late nineteenth century came to feel that American society was hostile to democracy and self-reliance. Among the writers in this group, Hicks named Lafcadio Hearn,

Hamlin Garland, Harold Frederic, Edgar Saltus, Stephen Crane, Edward Bellamy, and H. H. Boyesen. Hearn, Garland, Saltus, and Crane eventually departed from America. Bellamy in his utopian novels expressed rebellion; saw the possibility of an ordered, just industrial society; and exposed thousands of Americans to the idea of Christian socialism. The trouble was that Bellamy wrote from the point of view of the middle class and not of the workers, so that readers did not see the envisioned society from the workers' point of view; still, Hicks said, his novels were a valuable influence. Crane's value was in defying taboos that other writers would not; but, since he only felt the horror of war and poverty and did not understand their causes, Hicks considered Crane to be a symbol of the 1890s—of the talent that flares and strikes blind, bitter blows against evil, but is extinguished.

A group of novelists and journalists coming into print mainly in the first twelve years of the twentieth century did write more successfully about their own age and place, Hicks said, and these were the muckrakers and realists, among whom he listed Frank Norris, Upton Sinclair, David Graham Phillips, Robert Herrick, Winston Churchill, and Jack London. Although these writers treated important themes, Hicks concluded that their work was disappointing either because their fictional characters were not plausible or because they did not have a satisfactory (i.e., Marxist) point of view.

The young writers who represented the years 1912 to 1925 came mainly from the middle class, Hicks said, and they felt that class's loss of power. Optimism and pessimism were mingled in the attitudes of these writers, among whom he named Theodore Dreiser, Edith Wharton, Sinclair Lewis, Sherwood Anderson, Willa Cather, James Branch Cabell, Joseph Hergesheimer, E. A. Robinson, Amy Lowell, Carl Sandberg, Vachel Lindsay, Robert Frost, James Huneker, Joel Spingarn, H. L. Mencken, Irving Babbitt, Van Wyck Brooks, and Eugene O'Neill. These writers took two roads in seeking a solution to their frustrations: they isolated themselves from the masses of humanity and sought some haven, or they presented a more comprehensive portrayal of American society. Taking the road of isolation, Hicks said, had been Wharton, Cather, Hergesheimer, and Cabell—Wharton, by concerning herself with moral values and by writing of the socially elect class from which she came; Hergesheimer and

Cabell, by indulging in a combination of romanticism and affected pessimism; Cather, by indulging in nostalgic sojourns into the past after she had written her early vigorous novels about the pioneers of the prairie.

Dreiser, Anderson, and Lewis had taken the road of portraying the realities of contemporary society, and Dreiser had succeeded in showing the forces that worked through his characters in spite of his own confusions and pessimism. Anderson had successfully dealt with the effects of small-town life and the destructions of rural values by industry, and his recent interest in revolution, Hicks said, was a hopeful sign for him. Lewis had not joined the Communist cause, but he knew he wanted to destroy provincialism, complacency, and hypocrisy, although he had surrendered in late novels to the very standards he had satirized. These three writers, Hicks concluded, did not comprehend the forces of society; but they had made real advances in realistic technique that improved that of the muckrakers.

Poetry during this period had been vitalized by throwing off genteel restrictions and by expanding subject matter, an improvement that was evident in the work of Amy Lowell, Vachel Lindsay, and Carl Sandburg, for Robinson and Frost had dealt with limited worlds in their poems with some success. No poet, however, had conquered the new territory of the machine age, Hicks said; the period had produced many fine poems but no mature poet. The inadequacy of the critics dramatized the confusions of this middle generation, Hicks said, and the primary battle occurred between the impressionists like Spingarn, Huneker, and Mencken and the New Humanists like Babbitt, with no one providing a clarification of American culture. The impressionists at least encouraged writers to throw off conservatism, while the Humanists relied too much on religion and the past. Brooks did point to the money-mad spirit as the cause of failure of American literature but had not offered any social program. The pessimism and confusion of this period was reflected in O'Neill's plays, which expressed many kinds of frustration, Hicks said, but never arrived at a solution.

Writers after 1925, who turned away from society and took refuge in aesthetics, reevaluated the previous generation of writers as perhaps naive in worrying about such matters as provincialism. These new writers—secure in their middle-class assumptions that the existing social order, as stupid and hostile as it might be, was permanent—viewed literature as isolated from society and the artist as obliged only to cultivate and express his own sensibility. In this group Hicks included Joseph Wood Krutch, T. S. Eliot, Thornton Wilder, Ernest Hemingway, and William Faulkner, as well as critics Yvor Winters and R. P. Blackmur.

Finally, Hicks championed the new wave of writers with leftist political leanings that included John Dos Passos, Josephine Herbst, James T. Farrell, Erskine Caldwell, Albert Halper, Robert Cantwell, Jack Conroy, Edward Newhouse, Fielding Burke, Kenneth Fearing, Horace Gregory, B. Traven, John Howard Lawson, Clifford Odets, and others. This last group of writers implied in varying degrees in their writing the need for radical social change in America, and thus they promised, Hicks argued, to finish the journey which the dominant American writers had been traveling from the beginning.

Much of what Hicks said in the book is useful and informative even today, especially when it deals with the earlier periods; this work, however, has many faults. The value of it lies in the abundance of historical background and information about writers and movements. Much of this material, of course, was derivative; but it was put together conveniently and clearly. Although Hicks evaluated writers by the revolutionary yardstick, he tried to recognize the value of each writer's contribution. He maintained, however, that no writer had gone far enough in adopting a revolutionary world attitude, except contemporary writers in the radical movement of the 1930s mentioned above. Anyone interested in literary history can profit from the book, even if he rejects Hicks's insistence on the radical conversion.

On occasion in *The Great Tradition*, Hicks seemed to superimpose economic causes upon certain literary results, or he did not sufficiently prove the connection between economics and literature. For example, in talking of the writers after World War I, Hicks said that most authors belonged to the middle class that was being undermined by large industrialists. Capitalism was in its imperialist stage; the writers did not know that; but they sensed the debasement of the middle class. The sense of frustration of the writers of the middle generation was caused, according to Hicks, by the decline of their class. Their protest relied on individuals as an answer—a solution that could not stop the capitalists. Attributing these writers' troubles to the economic decline of their class seems an oversimplification, and Hicks offered little evidence to prove his generalizations.

Sometimes, Hicks did show that economic causes played a major part in certain results. He noted that the Southern agrarian poets, for example, were trying to turn back the tide of industrialism. This effort, Hicks said, was perhaps admirable, but it was quixotic. The young Confederates were ignoring the political and economic forces they had to contend with. They showed that their program was meaningless unless it could be founded on social and economic and political realities.

The fundamental Marxist scrutiny that Hicks used in examining American writers did shed some light on them. Such questions as what social and economic class a writer came from, how he regarded various social groups, and what his social assumptions were—or whether he dealt with social themes consciously or unconsciously—could provide some valid insights into the meaning of these writers. Certainly Hicks's is not the only possible approach, nor does it give as complete a picture as he thought. As we have noted, Hicks set out to prove his thesis that revolutionary literature was the culmination of the great tradition; and, although the value of that thesis is dubious, some of the social insights he presented are useful. For example, Hicks noted the failure of Mark Twain and Howells to analyze successfully the political realities of their times; Norris's failure to face the implications of the social problems he presented; and the shallow superman philosophy and racist preoccupations of London. Hicks erred, however, when he tried to explain the weaknesses of certain writers as due to their class alignments, as in the case of his treatment of Stephen Crane, of the muckrakers, and of James, Faulkner, and Wilder. Whatever faults can be found in those writers are not to be discerned simply by applying class labels. However, Hicks did effectively show that Thomas Bailey Aldrich stood for shallow, "middle-class" values when he pointed out that Aldrich wrote not only discreet (albeit well-wrought) trifles in verse but also portentous odes about the righteousness of the government and the superiority of the Anglo-Saxon race. It was, however, his shallow values and not necessarily his class alignment that was at fault.

In dealing with writers of the 1930s, Hicks too hastily rejected those who did not present life from the proletarian (i.e., leftist radical) point of view; for he did not consider how well Cather,

Faulkner, Wilder, and Hemingway depicted life. Because he
tried to milk every drop of worthiness that he could from the
work of leftist writers, the mystique of the proletariat led him
astray. Such an attitude from Hicks also indicates that he did not
realize that workers were a long way from being revolutionary in
America and, furthermore, that they ignored literature.
Culturally, they indulged in escapist entertainment. For the most
part, they blamed themselves for being out of work; and they
either tried to work harder or looked to the existing government
to relieve their plight, which eventually it did. The socialization
of production was a long way from coming, and revolutionary
literature was not to have the influence—at least not so directly
and immediately—that Hicks dreamed in this book that it would
have.

V   Figures of Transition

In the second half of the 1930s, Hicks conceived an ambitious
plan to apply his Marxian analysis to all British literature since
the end of the Victorian period. *Figures of Transition*, which was
not published until December, 1939 (two months after Hicks had
left the Communist party and four months after the Stalin-Hitler
pact of August 21), was his only book about British authors that
materialized before he became disillusioned with communism
and with Marxist criticism. Because of these circumstances,
Figures of Transition received little critical attention, but this
work is a better literary history and contains better criticism than
The Great Tradition. Its improvement is partly due to the fact
that Hicks covered fewer writers, gave more supporting details,
and was also less polemical.

Hicks first dealt with the Victorian period in England from its
time of full strength to its demise, as he saw it. His primary focus
was on considerations of the economic and political ideas of the
writers in regard to the working class. He divided writers into two
basic groups: those who in social matters favored utilitarian ideas
or were allied with the related evangelical spirit (related because,
he said, this spirit stood for piety, individualism, and frugality)
and those who opposed utilitarian ideas. The so-called utilitarian
ideas included such notions as the following: "the greatest good
for the greatest number," the possibility of "scientific" legislation
to bring about general material well-being, the elimination of

governmental interference in economics as much as possible, and the necessity of not pampering the poor in order to avoid over-population. Among the utilitarians Hicks listed Jeremy Bentham and those who embraced versions of his theories, such as Lord Brougham; and, among the evangelicals, Hicks named Anthony Trollope. The chief opposition to utilitarian ideas, Hicks said, came from Samuel Talyor Coleridge, Thomas Carlyle, Benjamin Disraeli, Charles Kingsley, Elizabeth Gaskell, and Charles Dickens; for these writers offered spiritual solutions for what they considered to be spiritual problems. These writers, who did not think the working class should take over and help govern itself, believed that the rulers of society had to be made to see and to understand the need for the improvement of the workers' lot, as well as the falseness and emotional narrowness of utilitarian ideas.

After the turbulent years of 1832 to 1848, labor unrest subsided, and the evangelical spirit prevailed. Soon, however, the evangelical spirit was undermined, Hicks said, by the discoveries of science and evolution that destroyed its theological basis and by writers like Matthew Arnold and George Meredith who attacked the commercial spirit, the prudery, and the smugness of the middle and upper classes. Hicks hastened, however, to recognize the richness of the literary output of this period; and he gave credit, in spite of their social views, to Carlyle, Alfred Tennyson, William M. Thackeray, and others. The middle class had established itself in the seat of power, and prosperity helped to reassure this group. But then prosperity declined, too, and insights were needed, Hicks said, into what was happening and why. The writers of the 1880s and 1890s had to cope with uncertainties of all kinds, economic, religious, and scientific.

Next came the rise of socialism, and Hicks championed William Morris because, Hicks contended, Morris's socialism was close to the Marxist and not the Fabian or romantic type. Hicks traced the battles in the rise of socialism and the workers' cause and showed that Morris was started on that road from John Ruskin's antiindustrial ideas, although Morris did not believe, like Ruskin, in a return to feudal society. As an artist creating and selling better home furnishings and as a writer of medieval narrative epics, two utopian novels, working-class songs, and light prose romances on medieval themes, Morris sought to clear the way for better art by improving society and had no high pretensions about his work. Capitalism was on the defensive, and reforms came, but Morris insisted that the workers would have to destroy capitalism eventually. In forceful, clear pamphlets and speeches, Hicks said, Morris exposed the vulgarity of the Victorian middle class and the antiliberty, imperialist feeling of many upper-class people.

Hicks attributed more importance to Morris than to Bernard Shaw and H. G. Wells, the leading Fabian writers, who believed in the gradual, peaceful transition to socialism with the middle class in the lead. "Morris could not be satisfied with less than Communism, and that was fortunate," Hicks concluded, "for many who could be satisfied with less deceived themselves into believing that they had got or were about to get all they wanted. . . . Morris was right on fundamentals and the Fabians simply not right at all."[11] Hicks did not explain what he meant by the Fabians not being right, which seems strange, since the program of the Fabians has come closer to what has happened in England than the predictions of Marx. Hicks apparently assumed that any concessions the capitalists had made would be lost later, for he thought capitalism would soon collapse—unless fascism prevailed.

The kind of optimism and serenity that Morris showed was rare for his time, Hicks said; for while Thomas Hardy was on the other hand more preoccupied with the question of an indifferent or unjust universe than most other thinkers were, most were bothered by the doubts raised by science. But Hicks gave Hardy credit for explaining the problems as an artist and for stating different speculations in different works, even though he was not a systematic philosopher. Hardy felt man was too sensitively developed to live happily in this world, but he *did* believe that men should work to alleviate social ills and harmful attitudes, and he had respect and sympathy for humans. He did not get much involved in fighting social evils, however, because of his personal shyness and sensitivity and the disappointments he had experienced as a young man. His pessimism was more a matter of experience, Hicks concluded, than it was of philosophy.

Hicks characterized Samuel Butler as a "cautious rebel" who bolted from the tyranny and orthodoxy of his father, who wanted the church to be a social institution, and who was concerned about the social consequences of unpopular views. Butler, who stumbled onto his now rejected theories about evolution and the role of unconscious memory, got into a battle with Darwin partly to assert himself rather than to advance science. He was a man, Hicks argued, who wanted to be the friend of such socially prominent people as high churchmen. Butler was a snob, Hicks said, who thought the rich swell was the epitome of what man had been striving for, and he concerned himself little with labor conditions or the working class. He satirized imperialism to some extent, but he never doubted the permanence of capitalism. He argued for the importance of money and expressed a utilitarian basis for morality. His fame rested, Hicks said, on his posthumously published *The Way of All Flesh*, for by 1903 many were ready to agree with what he said in the book.

Because the uses of, and the demands on, the British novel began to change from what they had been at the height of the Victorian period, Hicks observed that the writers demanded that they be allowed to use more realism, they argued that truth was the only justification the writer needed, and they rejected the demands of the ruling class. Morris, Hardy, and Butler had helped bring about new freedoms for writers. Then George Gissing and George Moore emerged to write of the lower strata of the population, each for different reasons and with different results. Here Hicks was warming to his favorite subject—"proletarian" writers. Gissing, who had grown up among the poor, knew the misery of their lives and could write about them from this knowledge. Although he wrote at first to protest about their conditions, as in *Workers in the Dawn*, his motivation was to escape from their disgusting lives by advocating social change. Gissing, who later escaped into a study of the classics and wrote confessional novels about his abandonment of social reform, as in his second novel *The Unclassed*, continued to write about the poor; but he wrote of them with either contempt or only moderate sympathy, and never from the point of view of militant workers. He expressed distaste for industrial civilization with its "brute force of money," but he wanted money and admired those who had it. What Gissing gave to the modern novel, Hicks said, was emancipation from Victorian taboos and the sense of possibilities in new themes.

Hicks then asserted that time had proved in America and in England that even a clumsy craftsman could reach the readers' imaginations if he was absorbed in his material and honest and patient. "We have been forced, almost in spite of ourselves, to respect saturation in the commonplace" (203). Gissing, he said, had been showing the way. Hicks was groping for a way, it seems now, to justify social realism and the work of revolutionary writers of his time. Not many critics would now hold that a dull, dreary realism poorly done is sufficient to hold our attention. Hicks treated Gissing objectively, however, and built his case for and against him with substantial examination of details.

George Moore, coming from the upper class, approached the novel of the lower class with motives inspired by the naturalism of Emile Zola, Hicks said, and he held his romantic tendencies in check in order to show his characters as products of their environment. His *Esther Waters* was remarkably modern as realism because of its objective presentation and its lack of sermons and comments to the reader that appeared in the novels by Gissing and most other Victorians. Moore proved, Hicks said, that the public would accept a truthful novel about the lower classes. Moore then turned to psychological novels, Hicks concluded, and he became self-conscious about style and wrote nothing of importance. Although Hardy, Gissing, and Moore had made beginnings in freeing the novel from bourgeois restraints, they had then forsaken the realistic novel; and they had done so, Hicks observed, because of their "sense of the difficulty of coming to terms with contemporary society" (216). Their successors, Hicks opined, would have to meet the problems they had turned away from.

Among other artists who were to have problems with society was Oscar Wilde; but, as Hicks said, he was more determined to make himself noticed than he was in championing any theory like aestheticism. Wilde became a symbol of decadence and of the aesthetic movement because of his self-advertisement. Since he represented a threat to Victorian institutions, he achieved the fame he wanted; but he was destroyed when, with overconfidence, he went too far in making his homosexuality public. The work of the aesthetes, Hicks argued, ". . . had always rested on a non-literary principle, that is, on hatred of the bourgeoisie. As Wilde's career has already made plain to us, the doctrine of art for art's sake was a protest against contemporary standards and a way of escaping from bourgeois controls" (259). The feverishness of their attack, however, resulted in a closer look at prevailing standards. Ultimately, they got their revenge on Victorianism, but they were ill-equipped for survival.

The late Victorian writers who contributed to disintegration, Hicks said, were met with anger, for the middle-class public wanted reassuring books. The new rise of imperialism, which had begun to decline at the end of the eighteenth century, along with the change from industrial to finance capitalism, gave the English middle class new optimism, Hicks said. And the two writers who gave them the assurance that they wanted were Robert Louis Stevenson and Rudyard Kipling.

Stevenson offered a shallow moralism but still a sense of honor, dedication, and courage. "To keep the old morality but rid it of asceticism, to defy the new despair, to disparage the gospel of respectability and success—that was Stevenson's aim" (268). Stevenson had had a brief flirtation with socialism, but he came to dislike the industrial society and longed for the preindustrial era. He could feel sympathy for courage and heroism, but he could not grasp the meaning of industrial growth and decay and exploitation or struggle against it. Late in life, when he went to Samoa for his health, he defended the Samoans against imperialist abuse and wrote a few things about the islands. His work on the whole was juvenile, Hicks concluded, and it lost its charm for the reader who had matured.

To Hicks, Kipling was the ideal spokesman for the Empire; he was a writer who grew up overseas as the son of a military father and who took for granted the ideals of serving the British Empire. His extraordinary talents showed themselves in the dozens of stories he wrote while a hard-working journalist in India and in his verses about military life in the colonies. When he returned to England as an established writer, he saw that the English were not aware of the importance of the holy mission of imperialism. As a result, he set about making himself the spokesman for it. His were not the ideals of avaricious capitalists exploiting foreign natives. He saw the Empire as a stern, God-given obligation to the English who were to civilize the world, to accept the "White Man's Burden." The natives of India were admirable in many ways, but they needed iron rule over them. All this talk of liberty and democracy and religious skepticism made little sense, Kipling said, when one was close to the harsh realities of life, as one was in India and elsewhere. Kipling was a didactic writer for the most part, Hicks observed, and he was poor at showing human relationships on any complex level. His strength came from his verbal skill and his early tales of life in India; and, without India, his well soon ran dry. He did not much mature as a writer, Hicks said, and in later years he was frustrated by the softness he saw in Englishmen as the capitalists became parasites amid luxury and the poor were, in his eyes, coddled.

With Victorianism dead and with changes in the economic system bringing prosperity again, Englishmen came to see, Hicks argued, that it was possible to tolerate changes in outlook and behavior that once would have been thought intolerable—as long as capitalism was preserved. Victorianism was dead; the writers were freed, Hicks said; but the newly confident Edwardians could have been told that the major problems still remained. "Finance capitalism was not a better basis than industrial capitalism on which to build a culture; the growth and the effects of parasitism proved the contrary." The Edwardians could never be more than post-Victorians, "an aftermath, not a beginning," Hicks concluded. "They, too, were figures of transition" (315).

Figures of Transition is a solid piece of literary criticism in which Hicks fulfilled his objective of relating social background to individual writers and their works. Implicit, of course, in his approach was the premise that capitalism had reached its height in the nineteenth century and had begun to decline and that socialism was on the rise. He examined these representative writers to catch any glimpses of socialist trends in them and to measure their attitudes toward the capitalist rulers and the exploited workers. In short, although he still had his "Marxist" point of view, he treated these writers fully and objectively by giving them generous credit for what *he thought* they had contributed. He built his case with impressive details, both from their backgrounds and from their literature. Perhaps it was easier for Hicks to treat these writers of another age and another nation with less passion, for he seemed to be less able to keep a balance in treating the current writers who were producing the books that he was reviewing.

In *Figures of Transition*, Hicks, in summary, showed the usefulness of asking the questions about class background, economic forces, and individual attitudes and motives. He asked pertinent questions about the attitudes of the writers, such as those of Kipling and Stevenson. He examined their works, we can say, as a humane moralist; and he succeeded in doing what he had done only superficially in *The Great Tradition*.

VI   *Some Evaluations*

The work that Hicks did during the 1930s was not worthless. Nevertheless, although much of it was useful and interesting, we must conclude that, by and large, his attempt at Marxist criticism was a failure. The essential ideas that Hicks advocated for literary analysis and evaluation show some strengths but also many weaknesses. First, his seeing society from the point of view of the workers did help to clarify many issues and to reveal many aspects of injustice for the person interested in human values. But Hicks wanted writers to portray the feelings of the "vanguard of the proletariat," that is, of the militant workers who were, in fact, largely mythical. As we noted in chapter 3, he wanted their books to convey a feeling of hope for the future rather than pessimism or futility. Many writers did not feel such hope, but they were able to portray social realities. Moreover, the effect of Hicks's urging writers to "become" militant proletarians could easily have led them to feel and to express emotions that were not spontaneous, and any lack of sincerity on the part of a writer usually results in a weakening of his art.

Second, studying the possible effects a literary work might have on its readers is a valid approach. If the critic thinks that the work promotes false or harmful values or attitudes, he is justified in saying so, especially if he can show specifically what assumptions the literary work implies. But Hicks narrowed this effect theory to considering what effect a literary work would have on workers being prepared for the revolution; and he wanted the effect to be direct enough to "galvanize" them into action. He expected literature's role to be much too direct in its effect, rather than to expand the reader's perceptions and sympathies in a general sense.

Third, studying the social and economic background and even the biographical facts about an author can help the critic to illuminate a literary work. And such knowledge can serve as a basis for evaluating the "truth" of the work, if the critic also uses such information for the exposure of prejudices and questionable assumptions. Whether the critic's looking at the forces and relationship of economic production gives the most insight is, however, an open question. Hicks argued that literature which did not reflect the economic conflicts in a society was either false or unimportant. Strictly defined, this limitation of the subject matter of literature leaves out a good many subjects that people are concerned with in poetry and fiction, such as the problem of death and a hereafter. The only point at which a Marxist critic, or any other kind of critic, should object is where he sees a distortion or falsification of the realities of economic conflict. Otherwise, the question of subject matter is the writer's choice, and ultimately that of his audience.

Finally, Hicks in the 1930s had a stern and almost puritanical approach to literature. As he talked about how literature should not foster attitudes that would be harmful for the proletarians in the difficult fight they faced, he forgot to say much about the pleasure one can derive from literature. While it is true that art was traditionally regarded from classical times through the eighteenth century as having a social purpose—as serving to instruct—it was also considered a source of delight. Samuel Johnson said, for example, that art was to "instruct by pleasing." Hicks seems to have been so caught up in the idea of revolution that he overemphasized its importance and underestimated the pleasurable aspects of literature—not merely "aesthetic" pleasure but also the pleasure of knowledge, humor, insight, vicariousness, and emotional release.

Perhaps the main problem with Hicks's type of critical approach was its preoccupation with social injustice. While it is true that literature that is frivolous or false in its treatment of the harsher facts of life is unworthy, an obsession with social wrongs leads to a limitation of vision and to a narrow or a humorless attitude toward life. Ideally, even social realism should present not only the suffering, the injustice, and the meanness but also the delights of human experience.

To examine the treatment Hicks gave to any specific writer during his Marxist period is to see the narrowing effect of dogmatism. In summary, Hicks often had important things to say about social background, politics, and philosophical attitudes expressed in literature. Although he often stated aptly what a writer's objective was, he also denied the value of, or expressed no interest in, many of the imaginative insights that literature affords. What Hicks had to say about literature or a specific literary work was only part of what could have been said, for he did not allow his faculties of appreciation to operate freely. Although Hicks later looked back on his Marxist criticism with a sense of regret and chagrin, rejected the Marxist literary principles he had formulated and thereafter adopted a flexible approach, and tried to analyze the failure of Marxist criticism, he never again formulated or had much relish for literary theory. He remained largely eclectic, impressionistic, and subjective during the last thirty-eight years of his career as a critic.

CHAPTER 5

Anti-Marxism and Later Social Views

AS a disillusioned Communist, Hicks suffered much embarrassment and had to do a lot of soul-searching. By his open and
honest statement of his views, he had made himself a public
symbol of the native American intellectual who had turned to
communism in the 1930s. His timely and symbolic resignation
from the Communist party was an historically significant gesture.
Since he candidly stated his disillusionment, he recovered credibility more quickly perhaps than he might have, but he still faced
a long struggle to gain reacceptance. In the years that followed,
Hicks wrote a great deal about both his literary and political
adventures with Marxism. Although he remained more or less in
the "liberal" camp politically, his social and political views
underwent several changes after his departure from the Marxist
viewpoint in 1939.

I *The Stalin-Hitler Pact*

Hicks tells in his autobiography of that fateful day in 1939
when Stalin betrayed the United Front against Fascism: ". . . on
the morning of August 22 . . . as I stepped into the kitchen, I
heard a radio announcer say that Germany and Russia had
agreed to sign a non-aggression pact. 'Jesus Christ' I said to
Dorothy, 'that knocks the bottom out of everything.' . . . I
realize now that I had had more doubts about the Soviet Union
and about the Party, too, than I had ever admitted to
myself. . . . What confronted me at the moment was the simple
fact that Russia was no longer in the anti-Fascist camp and therefore was not on my side."[1]

In his letter "On leaving the Communist Party," which was
published on October 4, 1939, in the *New Republic*, Hicks said
that he did not know what was going on in Europe, that he would
keep an open mind, and that he certainly wanted to see the rights

of the party protected. Because the American Communist party had been caught unawares and was trying to justify Soviet policy, the party leaders had shown, he said, "that they are strong in faith—which the future may or may not justify—but weak in intelligence." The party's effectiveness had been destroyed, Hicks said, although he still believed in socialism and would defend Russia's achievements. "I know as well as any party member that the pact is not the cause of the present drive against the party, and I know too that no progressive movement is safe if the party is suppressed. The whole progressive cause has suffered, and we must repair the damage as rapidly as possible. . . . I value my years in the party . . . for the opportunity they gave me of fruitful work for a cause I believed in. My problem now is how to continue that work."[2]

A year after his resignation from the Communist party, Hicks repudiated Marxism. He still called himself a socialist, but a democratic socialist. He soon lost his enthusiasm, however, for trying to formulate a new socialist party. He later came to call himself a "critical liberal." During the 1940s and 1950s, he rebuked communism and those liberals who defended it. In his first repudiation of Marxism in a 1940 essay, "The Blind Alley of Marxism," Hicks said that the ideas of Marx and Engels were faulty because they put too much emphasis on the unrest of the victims of capitalism as the source of its downfall and not any on the desire for a more just and more rational society, even though they themselves exhibited humanitarian motives. The revolutionaries came largely from the bourgeoisie, Hicks said, and this complicated the problem of motives, a problem for which Marxism offered no explanation. What was the source, in other words, of these values? Furthermore, Marx assumed that eliminating economic problems would solve all other problems. Although Marxism helped us to understand economic forces, ". . . when it ignores motives other than self-interest and class interests, even though its own existence cannot be explained in terms of such motives, we have a right to be suspicious."

Hicks said, further, that Marxism asserted that power had to be seized at all costs, but the question of what the power was to be used for was not answered. What happened was that a corps of professional revolutionaries took over and asked for blind obedience from the masses: "Only when they are in power, when, in other words, it is too late to do anything about it if they have betrayed you, can you clearly discern their intentions." The fault lay not only with Stalin, or anyone else, but with the Marxist concept of power and of history: "We cannot leave it to history, as Marx and Engels did, to put the brake on the misuse of power. . . . We want power for socialism's sake, not for power's sake, and if the Leninist way does not take us to that goal we must find another."[3]

II His Rejection of Marxist Literary Criticism

Hicks rejected Marxist literary criticism along with the political ideas. In "The Failure of Left Criticism," he explained the connection and the lack of connection between Communist politics and the leftist critics of the *New Masses*. No one had told him how to review a book or had ever changed his reviews, he said; but he still regretted the political connection. "By joining the Communist Party, I had committed my future to a group of politicians, and I ought to have kept a much sharper eye on them than I did." Two schools of leftist criticism had been at work, he said—one group emphasized general principles, economic forces, the class struggle, and so forth; and the other group talked of technical excellence in literature. In neither group were there critics who were "capable of consistent analyses and mature and well-rounded evaluation."

Leftist criticism, Hicks continued, was hurt also by the virulent arguments over politics and by the critics' notion that they were to use criticism as a weapon in the class struggle. Marxist critics had tried to argue that capitalism should be destroyed while, at the same time, they were evaluating literary works; this procedure was wrong, Hicks said, because "we were in no position to make our statements about the author and our statement about capitalism part of the same proposition." Leftist criticism had not been valueless but had been less effective than it could have been. The leftist critics not only had helped make people aware of the Depression and of the books about it but had also caused them to read with understanding such great books as Steinbeck's *The Grapes of Wrath* and Wright's *Native Son*. The critics were now less certain about many things and did not feel criticism could be a major weapon, but perhaps they could now go further and produce mature and balanced analyses of literature.[4]

Many years later, in 1969, Hicks made some significant

statements about his errors in criticism during the 1930s in the foreword and afterword that he wrote for a paperback reprint of *The Great Tradition*. He had not been an expert on Marxism, Hicks said, although he had tried to educate himself. By the time he had finished the book in 1933, he was "bold enough, and ignorant enough, to call myself a Marxist, but I knew in my heart that I was an amateur." He had come to believe that he had discovered a great revelation in the Marxist interpretation of history and that he could show America these great truths and advance social progress. "Such certainty is intoxicating and dangerous, and I hope that . . . my experience may be a warning. . . ."[5]

Marxism was useful for analysis, Hicks said, but not for evaluation. He still believed, for example, he had been right in *The Great Tradition* when he said that greed, cynicism, and vulgarity in the Gilded Age had had something to do with the weakness of post–Civil War literature and had caused writers to retreat to other times and places for their subjects. "I might have stopped there, as some others did, saying that Marxism was a useful instrument for the explaining of literary phenomena but had nothing to do with evaluating them. Thus one could say that, from a Marxist point of view, such-and-such was a very reactionary book but on literary grounds was very good indeed."[6]

Another of his misconceptions had been on the subject matter of literature. His major error, Hicks said, was in assuming that the proper concern of literature was "man-in-society." He had felt that way in the 1930s, not because of Marxist dogma, but because he was sure society was falling apart. He had not been interested in metaphysical or psychological problems, and "That seems to me pretty sad. Man's social relations are still the subject of much fiction and rightly so, but some of the greatest literature of our own as well as earlier times grows out of a concern with man's place in the universe, and the attempt to see the individual in depth, to examine all the selves, has inspired some of the most original work of our time."[7]

As for his evaluations of specific writers in the book, he had changed his mind about several of them. Walt Whitman, for example, did not seem to him as great as he had when Hicks had felt obliged to approve of him for political reasons. But much of Whitman now seemed "to be marred by a forced and false rhetoric." Moreover, he now found in Mark Twain the values he had not seen in the 1930s when he had charged Mark Twain with reverting to the past. "Now I am glad that he did; what he had to say about the human condition he said beautifully in *Huckleberry Finn*, and nothing else matters."[8]

Henry James, Hicks said, had been his greatest stumbling block, for he had seen James as not getting out of his class politically and as not writing about social subjects. He had judged James on his lack of social consequences, whereas he now felt that *enjoyment*, although it was not the only justification and use for literature, came closer to explaining its value than inspiring readers to *action*. "As an examiner of life, James was superb." And about Robert Frost he had also been wrong; he had insisted that Frost should write about industrialism. He had enjoyed Frost, but he had tried to pretend that he had not.[9] Furthermore, Hicks said, he now appreciated the experiments that William Faulkner had been making. And he had judged T. S. Eliot too much by his politics, although he had enjoyed Eliot's poetry and had known many lines by heart. "I never did accept his ideas, but *Four Quartets* came to seem to me one of the few great poems of our time."[10]

III   *A Liberal Anti-Communist*

During the 1940s and 1950s, Hicks wrote a great deal about communism and related subjects. At the same time, even though he was suspicious of the Communists, he spoke out against Mc-Carthyism and the persecution of ex-Communists. A good example of his later views about Marxism was expressed in his essay "On Attitudes and Ideas," which was part of a 1947 series, "The Future of Socialism," published in *Partisan Review*. In the essay, he outlined further the shortcomings of Marxism and defined his idea of critical liberalism. Marx and Engels had concluded that all history could be explained in terms of class struggles and that social and cosmic laws would bring about what they had desired from the start. Their preoccupation with historical processes was a great contribution to understanding, Hicks said; but they refused to define clearly what kind of socialist order was to be developed. We had, therefore, to reexamine not only the goals but also the means to be used to reach them.

When Hicks questioned whether or not capitalism was bound to collapse and whether the proletariat was its heir, he thought that what had happened was that capitalism had been weakened by a stronger government and that the leadership of workers had not come from those who were most exploited. The discontentment in the world, he said, was not merely originated by economic problems; there were also psychological and moral discontentments, such as the meaninglessness to workers of much industrial work and the questionable values of capitalism. The biggest tendency was toward totalitarianism, not the inevitable classless society; and socialists and liberals had to be concerned with controlling the bureaucracy that socialization made necessary.

Continuing in the article, Hicks suggested that the means and ends were not simple and that trying to make them all look simple led to disillusionment: "The kind of optimism that is worked up in Communist and neo-liberal circles makes straight thinking impossible. That is why the writings of certain religious authors— Toynbee, Niebuhr, Eliot—are so often more impressive than the writings of radicals and liberals. Orthodox Christianity at the very least presents a view of human nature that is not flagrantly at odds with the facts we have experienced in these recent decades." The article defined leftists, not as ex-Communists, but as persons with certain attitudes they held in common: they were "united in their profound dissatisfaction with existing society, in their realization that not only the intellectuals but all classes of people suffer from the defects of the social order, in their adherence to conceptions of the good life that have been evolved in the course of mankind's six thousand years of experience with civilization, and in their sense of personal responsibility for present and future." These attitudes, which made them leftists, also accounted for the fact that some were ex-Communists; for their views had made them susceptible to communism in the first place.

Hicks urged leftists to begin with self-examination and to define what kind of a good society they wanted. Such ideas, Hicks asserted, then needed to be brought into the open; they needed to be criticized and revised; and the results were to be used as criteria for choosing the means to reach them. Hicks said he was against intransigent radicalism such as that of Dwight Macdonald, who had been author and editor of *Partisan Review* in the 1930s and later founder of *Politics* and a critic of mass culture, because his kind of radicalism would accept nothing less than perfection. The "critical liberal," on the other hand, "thinks the

possible is worth achieving. . . . Although the critical liberal is
aware of the limitations of reason, he sees reason as our best
reliance. What the critical liberal lacks in the way of dramatic
boldness, he can make up for by persistence." Communication
between intellectuals and nonintellectuals was also essential
because attitudes had to be clarified before any discussion of new
political organizations could be useful. "If we can clear away
some of the moral and political confusion, a new party, if one is
born, may amount to something."[11] This *Partisan Review* article
was Hicks's most seminal discussion of radicalism.

Hicks wrote several other magazine articles; he published a
book on communism; and, from 1946 until 1958, he wrote the
yearly article "Communism" for the *New International Year-
books*. These articles were objective, but they showed clearly that
he was not fond of communism, for he often stressed the point
that Soviet Russia's policies were formulated for their own national interests and not for world revolution.[12] From the research
associated with his writings, Hicks prepared an important article
for *Harper's Magazine* in 1946: "The Spectre That Haunts the
World." In this article in which he analyzed the rise of communism, he stressed its being centered in Russia. He contended
that Communists were influential everywhere except in Great
Britain and in the United States. The world was turning to it, he
argued, not because of the Soviets but because of dissatisfaction
with the status quo and with social injustice. He called for a new
world order and for the acceptance of a spheres-of-influence
agreement with Russia in order to give the world time to resolve
its problems. The United States should not let the world's revolution in the distribution of wealth be taken over by the Russians,
Hicks said; for, if we did so, our giving that country such power
would be our own fault.[13]

During the early 1950s, when all the talk about the menace of
communism and the resulting rise of Senator Joseph McCarthy
and his Red-baiting followers occurred, Hicks tried to serve as a
moderating force. He agreed that Russia was a threat and that es-
pionage had to be counteracted, but he also argued that civil
liberties had to be protected. In "The Liberals Who Haven't
Learned," he argued that the overall effects of the statements of
certain writers, notably those for *The Nation*, was to give Russia
the benefit of the doubt and to express distrust of the United
States in matters of foreign policy. "If the pro-Soviet front has

any strength in America today, it is because there are still liberals who provide the verbal cloak of 'social betterment' that hides the nakedness of the brutal revolutionary totalitarianism that is the Communist aim."

Many American pro-Soviet liberals felt that it was better to favor Russia, Hicks continued, than to be duped by American reactionary forces. That argument had an air of plausibility, but it showed how little its proponents had learned. Anti-Communists, he admitted, "seem to assume that nothing matters but the defeat of Communism and that all anti-Communists are their friends, but if the past two decades teach any lesson, it is that the wrongness of one extreme does not prove the rightness of the other." When the pro-Soviet liberals asked how they could be wrong if they opposed Senator McCarthy, the answer, Hicks said, was "that on these scores they aren't wrong, but that doesn't make them right about much else."[14]

In that same year of 1951, however, Hicks attacked McCarthyism. In "Is McCarthyism a Phantom?" he repeated his assertion that those who attack McCarthyism often defend Soviet policy. But McCarthyism was beginning to stifle free expression, he said, because it was based on "ignorant anti-Communism." "Will anyone seriously deny that there is less freedom of speech in America today than there was five years ago?" he asked. He gave examples of school officials and professors who were being fired because of the pressure exerted by "professional patriots." He cited a symposium on communism at which no pro-Communist speaker was allowed; for, since such a speaker would not have converted anyone, his views should have been heard. "Certainly the American people have reason to hate and fear Communism, but undiscriminating emotionalism is always a peril."[15]

In 1954, when Hicks published his book *Where We Came Out*, he told of his experience with communism and explained again not only what he thought should and should not be done about it but why he also had hope for America. He had bet on the wrong horse when he had backed communism in the 1930s, and he explained that "The mistake that I and so many others made in the thirties . . . was in assuming that there must be a solution for the . . . problems created . . . by the depression . . . . We wanted to have the whole mess cleaned up once and for all. That is the kind of mistake that intellectuals are prone to make. . . . Today I regard with skepticism all dogmas—religious, social, political, or economic." He emphasized, furthermore, that Communists were not just more extreme socialists; they were reactionaries, he said, except in some of the slogans they spouted when it suited them.[16]

Long before Hicks published *Where We Came Out* in 1954, however, he had indicated his caution and skepticism, as well as a tentative hope. Many political commentaries that he had made during the 1940s and in the earlier 1950s illustrate his change in attitude. The radicals of the 1930s had lost a sense of certitude, he said in 1941 in "Communism and the American Intellectual." After leaving the Communist party, Hicks observed in 1941 that he missed being active; "but I have learned that doing something for the sake of doing something creates one of the most dangerous of illusions." He was not against action: "Action should grow, however, not out of the faith in the inevitability of socialism or anything else, but out of wisdom with regard to the issues and humility with regard to the outcome."[17]

This wariness of easy solutions and dogmatism was expressed in many comments Hicks made. He felt, for example, that Lincoln Steffens in his flirtations with Marxism had been dangerous, for Steffens, who had searched for *a* solution, had had an "absolutist impatience." Now (1952) the quest for certainty was being conducted by the conservatives who wanted to return to religious dogma or to "*laissez-faire*, hysterical Americanism." The lesson of Steffens was the danger of that kind of mind that, to Hicks, had not died in 1939, or in 1945. But there were also panaceas with liberal labels, although many persons had learned to be skeptical. Still, because they had *not* learned "to be critical in any bold, imaginative way," they might make Steffens's kind of mistake again.[18]

IV   His Complacency in the 1950s

At the end of *Where We Came Out*, Hicks expressed hope for America. He felt that the rise in the standard of living for more people was cause for optimism, despite the warnings from some thinkers about a mass-production society that was swallowing up individuality, forcing standardization of life-styles, and creating enormous pressures for a colorless conformity in every aspect of life. Throughout the 1950s and early 1960s, he was relatively complacent about American society; moreover, some of his comments in 1952 show that, while he was groping for a new view, he was content to deal with limited problems rather than with society's major evils and injustices. In a review of a book about the utopian quest, Hicks said he was not in the mood for utopias. Science had outdone many utopian dreams, but we still had war and no peaceful, stable society. Furthermore, we had revolted against the idea of *one* solution to social problems; for abuses of power had also taught us many hard-to-forget lessons. Hicks said he could not imagine trying to write a utopian novel (as he had done in 1940): "I want to deal, as I do deal, with small problems that are somewhere near my size; and the idea of prescribing for the ills of society even in the most tentative fashion strikes me as presumptuous. Like most people, I am fighting a defensive battle, trying to ward off evil, trying to preserve values that are left to us, not thinking of values that might conceivably be created."[19]

Hicks admitted that the health of the individual person was threatened by mass society, but he could not see any solution being offered by "intransigent radicalism." Reviewing the book *White Collar* by C. Wright Mills in 1952, Hicks said that Mills was clinging to a radical label and was not offering a program to solve a problem he raised—that of the white-collar, middle-class worker who was not doing anything to prevent the evils of a mass business society. Mass production would not stop, Hicks said, and the radical stereotyping of the middle class was preventing men from doing what they could to solve the problems of mass society. When Mills rebuked the intellectuals for turning from politics, Hicks countered that Mills had no practical plan; and, until he presented one, the intellectuals had to "make the most of the advantages, the loopholes, that have been found to exist or can be discovered. . . ."[20]

On this same theme, Hicks said in 1954 that Irving Howe's passion for nonconformity defeated or nullified his shrewdness. To Hicks, Howe's nonconformity was touched with a nostalgia for the old radical days; the radicals did have a bad time now; the trouble was that their dissent was not very impressive. The status quo was not as bad as Howe tried to show it as being, and there was also less conformity. The working classes in America, Hicks asserted, were fully conscious that they had never before been so well off economically. They were aware that the prosperity might not last; "but they are making the most of it while it does, and, if I can judge from my neighbors, their best is pretty good." Hicks agreed with Howe about some of the causes and consequences of conformity, but he argued that Howe had not achieved "a really searching analysis of our cultural and intellectual problems."[21]

A year later, Hicks again sounded an optimistic note when he asserted that America was not doomed because of its misuse of abundance. (Like many of us, however, Hicks later became less smug about wasting our abundance.) When discussing Vance Bourjaily's book *The Hound of Earth*, Hicks disagreed that America had used up its citizens' energy, was doomed, and was the world's first neurotic nation: "I think that the patient has a fair chance and that, if he doesn't recover, it will be a different disease that carries him off. No one ought to have supposed that the first nation to achieve abundance would know how to use it wisely, but abundance itself is a good thing, and I believe that, if we are given time, its goodness will be proved. What we have to worry about is the large possibility that we will not be given time."[22] Hicks probably was referring to the threat of atomic war, for the problem of pollution did not emerge until the 1960s.

V   *His Pessimism in Later Years*

By 1968, the war in Southeast Asia was escalating; President Lyndon Johnson was sending increased numbers of troops to Vietnam; and Hicks expressed a more tough-minded view of our society. Later, he became pessimistic. In speaking of a collection of essays by Archibald MacLeish, Hicks was skeptical of the author's reasons for defending academic freedom. MacLeish supported it because of his belief in the human mind, the worth of individuals, the power of truth to prevail, and the human future. "Maybe so, maybe not," Hicks wrote. "My own advocacy of freedom of speech rests on a more pragmatic base: I find freedom of speech good for me, and I am not willing to deny to others what I demand for myself. I am willing to assume the worth of all human beings, but some are worth a lot more than others. I hope truth will prevail, but I am not certain that it will, either in the short run or in the long run, whatever that may be. And the central fact of our time is that the human future may be very short."[23]

In 1973, contributing to the report of the Harvard Class of 1923, Hicks said he was not worried about the collapse of the economy but of Western civilization. "I feel as Lewis Mumford does, that the great powers of science and industry, so capable of benefitting mankind, have been turned in the direction of destruction and waste." He admitted that he behaved more like an optimist than a pessimist: "I am philosophically a pessimist but temperamentally—or glandularly or what have you?—an optimist. . . . It works in practice, and by and large I take pleasure in each day as it comes along."[24]

His pessimism had not abated by 1974; for, when asked if he were a progressive, Hicks replied that he was not: ". . . I am not in any sense an optimist. I don't believe that civilization is getting better and better. I think civilization is almost certainly going to crack up in not too long, say twenty-five, fifty, or a hundred years; that is, I think we are on courses that are going to destroy the human race." To Hicks, the threat of atomic war and especially the problems with the ecology were serious problems. He said that he could see no way to keep industrialized societies from ruining the environment and from wasting the world's resources. He also saw too much power in the American military, and he felt that America was moving toward dictatorship (in spite of the removal of President Richard Nixon from office, which he saw as a mildly encouraging event).[25]

VI *Hicks as a Social Philosopher*

As we have seen, Hicks modified his social philosophy several times during his long career. As a young man, he became a progressive liberal; during the 1930s, he developed enthusiasm for communism; disillusioned by 1939 with communism, he expressed for a while some support for democratic socialism during the early 1940s; but he soon decided to label himself a "critical liberal." In the 1950s, he adopted a mellow view of the status quo; but, in later years, he became a little pessimistic. Our first reaction to these changes might be to say that he blew with the wind—that he had no consistent philosophy. That observation would be true in one sense, although he did adhere throughout his career to a set of vaguely humane, rationalistic values. Hicks, who was dealing with some of the most basic and crucial social issues of modern times, was, no doubt, naive in his young years. But so were many, many other thinkers; for Hicks was, indeed, a reflector of the intellectual movements of his time. After he had shed his Marxist dogmatism, he kept an open mind; he was honest about his mistakes; he was candid and humble. Throughout his long career in which he played the role of social thinker, Hicks maintained a nobility of mind, and a sense of concern and high purpose. Hicks made, as a critic, a valuable contribution by grappling with the problems of our civilization and by discussing books and ideas with candor. Whether his pessimism in his later years was a product of old age remains to be seen; but we realize that very grave problems face our world. However, since we have moved ahead of the story of Hicks's literary career, we must return now to the 1940s.

CHAPTER 6

Novels and Essays on the Small Town

HAVING been chastened by his disenchantment with communism, Hicks directed his interests in the 1940s from national and global affairs to local ones. Like everyone, he followed the events of World War II; but he focused his attention on the small town of Grafton, New York. He had largely given up any ambitious plans for literary criticism; but he continued to review books and write about literature from time to time (see chapter 7). He concentrated primarily, however, on writing novels built around his experiences with his fellow townspeople and with friends who lived in small New England towns. He also wrote a utopian novel and a nonfiction book about his observations, and he contributed several essays during subsequent years on the problem of the small town in an urban society.

I The First to Awaken

Hicks had been thinking of writing a novel even before his break with communism, and the radical publishers Modern Age Books wanted something from him. When he could no longer support communism, he still retained a vision of a future socialistic arrangement. From this idea came his utopian novel of 1940, *The First to Awaken*. This novel is a kind of author-transition work, for it reflects Hicks's social concerns as well as his turning to an interest in small-town life. Although Hicks wrote the book himself, he had a collaborator in Richard M. Bennett, an architect whom he had met at Rensselaer and who furnished futuristic drawings to go with the book and who also contributed some of its ideas. Like Edward Bellamy's *Looking Backward*, Hicks's novel tells the story of a man, who, after having slept a hundred years, awakens. The character, George Swain, is a bank teller in Braxton, a town similar to Troy, that is located in upstate New York.

As the novel begins, World War II is about to erupt, Swain's wife Elsie has died, and a local strike and the abuse of the workers have appalled him. A doctor who sometimes joins a tavern discussion group with Swain offers to put him to sleep when the bank teller remarks that he would like to skip the bad years that are ahead. Swain gladly accepts—and wakes up in 2040 attended by a nurse and finds himself in a new world. The citizens of this world know about his situation, since the doctor has left good instructions; and they also know that other such sleepers are to awaken in various parts of the world.

The world Swain finds is socialistic; in America, regional cooperatives are the basic forms of government; Europe had gone socialist first; Russia has recovered from its tyranny, and Stalin has been discredited in history as a monster. Although a Fascist dictator had assumed power in the United States after the war because of a depression, this Fascist president had been unable to stop a populist movement in the Midwest and West. Civil war had been mostly prevented, and the populace in the East had been won by example. Swain is told the history of how it all happened, but he also sees great technical advances in buildings and homes; he sees cars guided by beams, small flying machines, throwaway clothes, and medical examinations conducted while the patient sits in a room undisturbed. Little religion is left, although there is some. People are not coerced, even to save their health; they can ruin it if they choose. And they can live outside the cooperative communities in the old ways; however, few do so. News accounts are unsensational, and any opinions are expressed on different ratio stations and in different publications from straight factual news. When Swain had awakened, no curious reporters had bothered him, for everyone believes in respecting a person's privacy.

Since Swain sees many flaws in the persons he meets, he concludes that this new society is not a perfect but a sensible one in which privacy exists but not isolation or lack of community concern. There are no town-gown feuds in college communities. The idea of commercial advertising is laughable. The students look back at the history of the America with poverty amid plenty as absurd. They have not landed on the moon, but they are in no hurry to do so. When Swain himself goes around the world, he visits in one moving scene the site of a World War I battle in which he had fought.

Swain is characterized as a quiet, unassuming man somewhat like Hicks himself. He is no zealot but is sensitive and a little sad, reflecting very well the mood of his creator at this time. He attacks his own era as having been a mean one when he perceives that the students he talks with look too serenely upon it. They find the ideas of believing profit-motivated business men and of letting business alone as laughable, as not to be taken seriously. Having been reared under socialism, they do not understand what capitalism had really been.

In long talks with Simeon Blake, a vigorous and wise aged man, Swain learns that many problems still need to be solved and that happiness is an elusive quality that is still hard to define. But Blake agrees that physical misery is definitely worse than mental anguish. Swain insists he sees more happy people than he had seen in 1940: "You don't know how many men and women got warped and twisted by the society I grew up in. I don't mean merely the jobless and the underfed." As Swain admits, "I'm talking about men and women in my own class. Liars, toadies, bullies. That strike I've talked about so much; I can't make you see what I learned from it."[1] He mentions ministers, editors, doctors, and bank clerks who behaved evilly toward the strikers and who must have hated themselves and all humanity. Blake agrees and sympathizes with Swain, but he insists that people still have disappointments, for death and human limitations still exist. Death, still a sad thing, is perhaps more tragic because life is better than it was. When Swain wishes he could go back and see socialism come about without all the hardships that accompanied it, Blake replies that such progress always has to overcome problems and resistance. Swain says he knows but cannot be blamed for wanting to change it. Thus, Hicks is stating his message: he wants his novel to change people, but he does not think it will.

The book has a message, but Hicks does not shout it or exhort it as he had in the 1930s. The tone of the novel is listless, sad, sensitive, and tragically wise; the reader sees the point and feels the poignancy in George Swain quite well. In fact, Swain is such an interesting, convincing creation that we understand why he does not hesitate to be put to sleep. When he awakens, Swain finds new friends and is happy in a quiet, humble way. In the end, he decides it is time for him to go to work and perhaps find a wife. He takes a job as playground supervisor.

The novel expresses a tenderness for children, an approval of local community involvement, an advocacy of regional control, and a dislike of New York City that reflects Hicks's views. He wanted to turn inward to little things that he could handle, like local affairs; yet he wanted to say something about injustice in the world and his sadness about it. As a result, Swain expresses a sadness and a tragic serenity that is probably unusual in a utopian novel. As prediction, the book is faulty, of course, as all such novels must be. For example, there was no depression after World War II but an improvement in the standard of living. A utopian novel is seldom a blueprint for the future; it is always a provocative protest of the present. And as the protest of a sadder but wiser man, Hicks's Utopia is very effective. Yet the novel did not sell at all.

II   Only One Storm

Two years later, however, Hicks published a novel that did sell well, *Only One Storm* (1942), which was the first book to exploit fully Hicks's knowledge of and interest in the small town. At the ·same time, he drew upon his radical experiences of the 1930s. His main character, Canby Kittredge, leaves his advertising job in New York to run a print shop in his hometown in New England. Although radically inclined, he chooses not to join the Communist party. He does, however, print some circulars for strikers in a nearby city. He becomes involved in town politics and is elected to the town council—as a Democrat, which has seldom happened. The novel deals with his and his wife Christina's adjustments and trials in coping with the local community and with their intellectual friends, one of whom is a Communist, and from whom they become alienated because of the Stalin-Hitler pact. The novel depicts many other local people and other complicated relationships among the citizens.

One basic idea that Hicks presents in *Only One Storm* is that one must reconcile oneself to the limitations of humanity while at the same time maintaining one's hope for human progress. Another is the importance of doing the little things like working for one's community and developing a variety of friendships rather than being isolated with other intellectuals. Hicks presents the warmth of the community without being sentimental about the townspeople, for he also depicts their narrowness and meanness, and draws distinctions among them.

The novel ends with the funeral sermon for Old Henry Carter that is being preached by the deposed liberal minister Perry Bradford, who speaks of the need for prophets. The old man was a solid citizen, he says, but not the kind of prophet needed for the changes and hard times ahead: "The world is in chaos. Perhaps for a little while longer we can go our ways, but not forever," Perry tells them. "We too are part of the old order that is collapsing. We must have prophets or the people perish." This statement, which reminds Canby of an earlier conversation, enables him to shake off a doubt: "The phrase recalled to Canby Ralph Baxter's quotation about the people also perishing where there is vision, and for the first time he understood and was appalled by the emptiness of its cynicism."[2]

All the problems Canby has confronted are resolved in his mind as he listens to the sermon. He has worked through a number of moral and intellectual problems and has established himself and his family in the town. He is reconciled with his Communist friend Wallace, who has left the Communist party but is now alone to work out his destiny. The novel convincingly brings together at the end the uncertainties and ambiguities that Canby had felt. He is ready to go forward with his life in good cheer:

As the prayer ended and he lifted his head, Canby looked full into Christina's face, and he saw the tears in her eyes. Warm as her feeling had been towards Old Henry, her grief, Canby knew, was not for him. It was a vaguer sadness than that, and yet there was in it no stain of sentimentality. No one faced the evils of the world, actual and potential, with more courage or with a more realistic humor. But for the casualties of the human struggle she had unfailing sympathy. Her tears were for the pathos of Old Henry's vanity and the cruelty of Perry's courage. They were for Canby and for herself and for Wallace. They were for all Pendleton, with its meanness and its magnificence.[3]

The novel has a grass-roots appeal, for it is about a man who has turned from alien ideas about saving America and has chosen to work within the framework of the American traditions. Hicks tried to present in *Only One Storm* a more complicated narrative with a broader cast of characters than he had presented in his utopian novel. He had succeeded, but he had not found enough control of his narrative and was prone to present long conversations rather than action.

The narrative moves slowly at first; it is awkwardly written in many places; it has many wordy passages. The narrative point of view, which shifts often and awkwardly, is sometimes troublesome. The passages told from Canby's point of view are the best. But, in spite of the patches of poor style, the novel does portray many aspects of a small community; and, in a less interesting way, it depicts the dilemmas of liberal intellectuals who are coping with the issues of the late 1930s and early 1940s. The novel's reception was good enough to prompt Hicks to write another. This time, he was determined to produce a tighter and less discursive book.

III   Behold Trouble

Behold Trouble, which was published two years later in 1944, is a more successful novel than the previous one in depicting people in a small community, located this time in upstate New York rather than in New England. The supposedly central theme of the book causes some ambiguities: the protagonist Pierre Mason is a conscientious objector who ironically chooses to resist violently rather than go to war. Pierre, who is the son of a late local sheriff, suffers from psychological problems over his relationship with his father and from difficulty with people in general. The novel makes it clear that not all conscientious objectors are like Pierre—that some go to work in a special camp or serve in noncombat duty—but the issue of pacifism is somehow uncompelling. As a novel of ideas, the book is unsatisfactory. Hicks was struck by the irony of a pacifist's saying, "Come and get me!" and of his being willing to have a violent gun battle with police. (He had read of such a case.) However, his depiction of Pierre's mind at work is well done in spite of the muddied issue of pacifism; for Pierre is convincingly portrayed as a strong-willed and intelligent but confused person. Pierre kills a trooper and is himself killed in a climactic gun battle in the mountains.

Several other characters are drawn very well: Pierre's reticent wife Jenny, who suffers patiently with Pierre and who experiences an awakening during a night of sex with hillbilly hunter Carl while she is waiting in her cabin for Pierre to be brought home dead or alive from his mountain cave hideout; Mrs. Weisman, the elderly Jewish woman who rents a cabin from parsimonious, lecherous old Mel Tucker (formerly the "town bull"); Luke Tucker, who leads the air-raid wardens on a vigilante hunt for Pierre. These and other characters are skillfully and convincingly presented; and, when Hicks again shifts the narrative point of view from one character to another, he executes it very well. In fact, his handling of the thoughts and feelings of the characters could be compared favorably with the method of Henry James. In addition, the action of the manhunt and gun battle is told tersely and excitingly, with convincing, concrete details. Hicks displayed a thorough knowledge of the townspeople and their reactions to a person like Pierre, as well as of the surrounding mountainous countryside. There are, however, a stupid and promiscuous granddaughter of Mel Tucker named Flora who may be a bit too primitive and a newspaper reporter who is stereotyped.

When the action of the manhunt is over, the novel falters. It ends in a triangular conversation between Karen Bissell, her physician husband, and her old beau, who is now an agent for the Federal Bureau of Investigation. As they talk about Pierre, pacifism, and the war, Karen represents the more liberal, compassionate view. This chapter seems far removed from the central events of the story; and, as a resolution to the plot, it is too anticlimactic since the main action is over and since the conversation is relatively uncompelling. Hicks, who is back to an earnest discussion of ideas among middle-class intellectuals, has tried, as in the previous novel, to cover too much. The theme of pacifism is a distraction in the novel from its real value as a depiction of people in a community and their conflict with a dissenting, alienated, emotionally unstable young man. It is, however, the best-written novel of the four that Hicks published. The novel was not popular during those war years, although it did go into a second printing.

IV There Was a Man in Our Town

Hicks wrote another novel after he had finished his nonfiction study *Small Town* (see below); his *There Was a Man in Our Town* was finally published by Viking Press in 1952 after Hicks had left Macmillan and after some insistence by Viking's editor Malcolm Cowley that it be revised. Originally, Hicks had proposed *The Prickly Pear* as the title; and he observed in 1974 that he wished the original title had been kept.[4] Although this novel convinced Hicks that he had no great promise of success with fiction, it is a creditable book. It captures—perhaps better than his other novels—the flavor of small-town life and manners. The "man" in the town is newcomer Ellery Hodder, a professor of sociology who turns his attentions from abstract studies of cities to a practical reformation of the small town of Colchester. But the story is told by Bert Shattuck, a would-be playwright whose Uncle Will runs the town and whose Uncle Gary manages the charming old family inn where Bert stays when he is not in New York. The central theme of the novel is that a gap exists between theory about society and reality—a reality that flies in the face of theories. Ellery learns that the town is neither so susceptible to change nor so easy to manipulate as he had thought it would be, and he learns a few lessons about human nature, as well as some lessons in politics.

Another conflict in the novel is Bert's struggle to come to terms with himself, his family, and the town—by remaining aloof from them and by establishing his own identity. But Bert's conflict with his family and within himself is a distraction and is, at any rate, unconvincing because it is so tentatively dealt with. The novel might have been better if Bert had remained only a detached observer whose problems were omitted. From a technical viewpoint, he works well as the narrator, for he has both the intellectual equipment and the association with sophisticated society to understand and sympathize with Ellery, as well as enough familiarity with the town to see that Ellery is in for some disappointments as an outsider who is trying to be an insider.

The social events and the manners of the townspeople in *There Was a Man in Our Town* are interestingly depicted. Among such descriptions are a good scene in a tavern on Saturday night, another about a meeting of the fire company (at which Ellery creates a sensation by telling the members how he can obtain a donated fire truck), another describing a town social dinner, one on a fire, and one about an election campaign in which unscrupulous and malcontented Link Curtis wrecks Ellery's election plans. Ideas are discussed in this novel, this time with more narrative ease and plausibility than in the previous two novels. Politics is people, not programs, Ellery learns. He also comes to see that the social interrelations among a group of humans are complicated and that getting any group to work together for very long is very difficult. Ideas that are expressed in conversation and dramatized by events in the novel indicate that many people are mean, lazy, and unreasonable; yet they often are good, and they are always interesting. The manipulations of Bert's Uncle Will, the town despot in many ways, are seen as not being necessarily all bad; and Uncle Will, who proves to be more flexible than expected, is even interested in what Ellery Hodder might do for the town in the long run—although Uncle Will is not above resorting to expediency in an immediate situation to maintain his political hold.

One of the foils in the story is an overbearing woman sociologist in New York who wants to hear about her hero Ellery Hodder and about how he is doing in that quaint little town. She is all theory and condescension—and, to Bert, a horror. At the end, Bert, who is back in New York City, must again endure her at a party; but he answers:

> "It's the battle of the century. Ellery Hodder versus the Town of Colchester. The first round was a draw." I had behaved in the same childish fashion at Madeleine's party; apparently it was the effect Miss Balivet had on me.
> She didn't seem to notice. "It's so interesting. All over the country there's a movement back to the small towns. Housing shortages, the increasing tensions of urban life—"
> "Fear of the atom bomb," I added.
> She nodded gravely. "Now the question is: what are these trained, cultured men and women going to do to the small towns?"
> "And what are the small towns going to do to them?" I said.
> "So it's really wonderful that a man with Doctor Hodder's equipment should be making this kind of pioneer experiment."
> She went on and on. . . .[5]

Hicks was not one of our great American novelists, but he did write four interesting novels. He tried to present a true perception of the life around him and his feelings about it. Minor novels such as these by Hicks will be more valuable in the future than they seem now. Their insights into social behavior were worth expressing—and are worth preserving.

V Small Town

Hicks used his experiences with his village even more successfully in his nonfiction book *Small Town* (1946), for it is a work which should rank high on the list of anyone concerned with life in a small community. Studying informally the function-

ing and attitudes of the fictional village Roxborough, which is
based on Grafton, New York, Hicks described in detail this one
town—population, eight hundred—and put it into the context of
society at large. The result is an engrossing book.

First he described a typical day as he might have spent it,
established his purpose, and admitted his biases. He wanted to
tell the story of an intellectual in a small town, Hicks said, but he
did not want to separate the two. He desired also to indicate that
he mistrusted the city intellectuals when they talked of "the people," that he felt large cities were monstrous places to live, and
that they represented much of what was wrong with our society.
Furthermore, he argued, places like Roxborough were not mere
vacuums or "lags" in urban knowledge; instead, they were places
with positive advantages and were worth preserving for their
value to humanity. But his main purpose, he asserted, was
description, not argument.

Hicks discussed the crucial isolation between the intellectuals
and the remainder of the citizens of the communities in which
they live. To feel one is a part of a group of intellectuals (as Hicks
said he first had at Smith College) was to begin that fateful isolation which he now felt had been damaging both to himself and to
society. There had been, he admitted, amiable relationships between the citizens of Northampton, Massachusetts, and Smith
College. And the intellectuals were probably right about, for instance, the Sacco-Vanzetti case; but ". . . the fact remains that
the intellectuals had no chance of convincing the citizens because
they couldn't talk to them."[6] Hicks had felt as if he were an outsider—that he belonged, as John Dos Passos had put it, to another
nation. This situation, Hicks argued, was not the way it should
be, although he admitted during the course of the book that
nonintellectuals may never fully understand intellectuals.

Hicks was concerned about whether or not intellectuals could
be used for the betterment of society since, by and large, they
clung together and isolated themselves from other people. "I am
willing to defend two propositions. First, the isolated intellectual
pays a price, and what he gets may or may not be worth what he
pays. Second, the already calamitous situation of our society can
only deteriorate further if the gulf between the intellectuals and
other people continues to widen" (269).

The question of whether the intellectual should or could par-
ticipate was not easy to solve, for Hicks recognized that such a

person who could often contribute to his community in limited ways could be discouraged: "He will quickly discover, for example, that the majority of the people are interested only in their own affairs and have little concern for the common good. He will learn that most public issues are confused by factionalism, prejudice, stupidity, and a most unenlightened selfishness" (273). Hicks was certain that an intellectual like himself would not be a good leader. He could help clarify issues and suggest what to do, but he would be unable to convince the farmers and mechanics to *do* anything.

He thought that intellectuals were better able to cope with social forces and with other humans than many of the townspeople, although in many situations intellectuals were the ones who were helpless. They could express themselves, however, and could better understand the world outside the town. Often, personal grudges entered into public issues, and whether a townsman would be willing to help with a community even might depend upon what person asked him to do so. Hicks admitted that urban intellectuals were, however, less influenced by personalities in deciding issues than were the small-town people. "On the other hand, I am quite convinced, as I have already intimated, that the more perceptive and thoughtful of my neighbors have a better grasp of human realities than most of the intellectuals have. They know so many more kinds of people, and they know them in so many more ways!" (110).

After tracing the history of the village and of his house, Hicks talked of the town's "memory," which he found to be interesting and comforting, even though such towns were losing much of their identity because of consolidated schools, faster communication and transportation, and the many men who began to commute to factory jobs. The significant thing in the town was what Arnold J. Toynbee called "the link of locality," Hicks said, although jobs were often not tied to the town as they had been in the past. A self-sufficient small town of the past would have had many unifying ties among its people which did not exist in a city even if the inhabitants had lived together a long time: "I do not doubt that a man can be deeply loyal to a city of fifty or a hundred thousand, perhaps to a larger city, but it is not the same thing as the feeling of the townsman for his town." But Hicks admitted that the ghosts of the town's past were not always benevolent: "There is intense clannishness, suspicion of outsiders,

hostility to new ideas, resistance to change" (99). But if this
passage describes what the town is, he said, one can also see what
it once was and what it might be in the future.

Hicks also discussed the two social classes in the town, which
were not based on income but on some subjective judgment of the
townspeople. There was an "upper" and a "lower" class, but in
many activities, Hicks observed, few distinctions of even this kind
were made. "Although I still find it hard to believe, I am pretty
well convinced that class divisions in Roxborough are largely subjective. That is, a person by and large belongs to the class he
wants to belong to" (95–96). The so-called "upper" group
generally were more prosperous and aware of respectability,
Hicks said, but the group had been stretched to take in four men
who were poor, lazy, and drunkardly. Some impoverished people
asserted that they belonged to the lower class out of defiant pride.
"Another and larger group seem to be quite satisfied with their
lower-class status and are not sorry to be free from the responsibilities a higher rank might entail. They range from squalid
ne'er-do-wells to rather picturesque ruffians, men who enjoy
their drink and their fights and their women" (96).

One of the fascinations of the book is Hicks's observations on
the attitudes and mentality of the townspeople. The people
thought more about their own problems, he said, than about
social issues, books, or cultural affairs (except their own
folkways). Much of what the citizens talked about revolved
around farming, both practical lore and superstitions, which they
knew and discussed without ever indicating whether they believed them or not. Although they talked about the weather and
the beauties of nature, they also thought about, talked to, and
observed others in the town. Since radio was virtually the only
outside entertainment and since impersonal events and activities
were fewer than in larger communities, the townspeople were
more interested in others around them; but this interest in others
was not free from "emotional overtones."

Roxborough men kept themselves detached from the social
groups that industrialism had created, Hicks said, such as both
labor unions and management; and they often sought jobs that
gave them independence. However, they were very much interested in and knowledgeable about machines, particularly
automobiles; but, since such machines had been "domesticated,"
they did not threaten, as yet, their way of life. Another important

topic among the men was hunting, an appealing holdover from the older way of life. Most men and women said (when they were surveyed by Antioch College students) that they read newspapers and magazines, but few read them very thoroughly or with much sophistication. They took what they wanted from the radio and the periodicals and ignored the rest.

Hicks felt that the townspeople's knowledge of philosophy and religion had probably deteriorated during the previous fifty years. Most churchgoing Protestants were fundamentalists, but these and the "modernists" in religion probably represented only a fifth of the citizenry, for many people openly expressed little interest in religion or in going to church. To Hicks, a deterioration in practical morality had occurred: "I am not sure to what extent principles of conduct were ever a subject of intellectual consideration and discourse, but I am sure that in the nineteenth century there was general agreement as to what was right and wrong" (124). Although a new tolerance existed about such matters, Hicks thought it was a sign of growing confusion: "People are increasingly tolerant . . . not only of deviations from strict monogamy but also of falsehood, malicious scandal, political chicanery, law-breaking, and sharp practice. The development of new situations, for which the old standards prove inadequate, seems to have undermined those standards, so that they are not applied even where they are relevant" (124).

Political and socioeconomic thinking had also deteriorated. Although most people had a vague awareness of the complexity, size, and geography of the United States, they had been given by World War II some awareness of America's role as a world power; but this knowledge might have declined after the war. The Depression had changed few opinions about the value of free enterprise, and unionism was still regarded unsympathetically. Many ideas and areas of thought that a person like Hicks would be interested in were alien to the townspeople, such as music, novels, and pure science (for example, biological interest in the area).

"Human nature, Roxborough style," was not always encouraging; many admirable people could be found; but the town was a complex of "mysterious grudges and unspoken grievances." People often dodged responsibility, were afraid of criticism, and criticized those who took responsibility for town affairs. Some needed to be flattered to be persuaded to help; others worked willingly and quietly; but newcomers often led activities. Many of the younger people were inarticulate in the face of a more complex society; they often adopted an attitude of apathy or resentment and felt that they were being abused, which they either endured quietly or remained "perpetually sore" about. Most of the townspeople, however, were philosophical about economic hardships or natural disasters. The town also had its neurotics, for neuroticism was not confined only to urban middle-class people. Hicks said he was not qualified to determine whether small-town life contributed to various maladjustments: "I can only observe that we have our neurotics, our drunkards, our law-breakers, our 'bums.' And what is more, we know we have them" (152).

As for the many good traits in the townspeople, he had come to have greater respect for certain personal qualities, some of which he had once neglected: physical courage, manual dexterity, and loyalty. But intelligence was a quality for which he had acquired an even higher respect, whether he found it among townspeople or elsewhere. Above all, Hicks liked the neighborliness of the people, and, because of it, Hicks felt that he had acquired a broader understanding of and interest in people. A few he liked greatly; a few he disliked, and some merited his disapproval; but no one was "a blank, who existed for me merely as a function or a type. Good, bad, or indifferent, they are there—forces, dynamos, or more accurately, entities . . . human beings" (163).

The argument that books about small-towners proved these people were subhuman was not valid, Hicks asserted; for most people everywhere were probably much like the small-towners beneath their city clothes and language. "Aside from the special qualities, good and bad, of the old-timers, the human material in the town is probably pretty close to the norm. . . . I have never caught sight of the 'common man,' but I have watched the behavior of a certain number of specific men and women in specific situations, and I am not convinced that what I have seen is unrepresentative" (218).

Hicks described the town governmental bodies and other institutions: the township form of government, the school system, the fire district, the three churches, the Parent-Teacher Association, the wartime Defense Council (which later became the Community League), the library (which he had helped found and build), and the two political parties. He explained how the town's leading politician, who was their representative in the county, operated with and against other groups. He described how elections generally worked in the town, and how such a job as the road superintendent's was fought over. Often, he said, town office holders were incompetent, and petty corruption and stupid partisanship existed. People were dismayingly easier to exploit, Hicks concluded, than they were to help. Often, young persons who were potential good leaders moved away, and the town could probably have done better with one or two good leaders.

Education, or at least schools, did interest the people; but they left too much to the schools in preparing their children for the new ways of life different from that of their parents. The schools were not performing notably well, Hicks thought, for many of the unschooled oldtimers seemed better informed and clearer in their thinking. "Whatever education may do, it does not provide a background for ideas or create a medium in which ideas can thrive" (132). To Hicks, the high schools were not educating very well; they were, however, providing a social environment for teenagers, and that had some value. Vocational education was failing, Hicks felt, since the skills could either be learned quickly on the job or they were too complex for high-school students. As a school trustee in the township, Hicks had carefully studied the educational process and had concluded that children required better social studies if democratic planning and democratic understanding were to survive the threat of dictatorship. Education's burden was heavy, and the problem had to be attacked on several levels, not just in the schools. But, if the schools did their jobs a little better, that would help, he concluded.

To Hicks, as we have said, smaller communities seemed healthier in many ways than large cities. Most of humanity's past had been spent in them, probably with better results. "One thing at least is certain: the small-towner of a hundred years ago was better equipped for the life he lived than is the city dweller of today for his life" (214). Hicks realized that cities would not be abolished and that not everyone could live in towns the size of Roxborough: "To me the future of the small town is not a negligible matter. I know that the choice does not lie between cities like New York and towns of eight hundred. I have been happy in cities of twenty-five thousand, and I will even admit that a city of a hundred thousand—I would scarcely go higher than that—can offer opportunities for the decent development of the human being as a social animal" (217). Towns of five thousand, at least in the Northeast, might be ideal.

Hicks confronted the problem of preserving democracy and

preventing totalitarianism—and their relationships to the small community. He felt that somehow participation by people in the affairs of their local area had to be encouraged and developed. He had given up on socialism and was willing to accept capitalism as long as some participatory planning could be shared with it. He expressed fear that the experts would take the shortcut methods which would lead to totalitarianism, for, in revolutions, the minority of experts had the power, not the people. He was concerned, therefore, that democracy be preserved along with planning; and for this reason he advocated that planning for a region should include democratic participation. When he discussed the Tennessee Valley Authority as a possible example, he admitted that the people of that area probably did not feel it was their project (even though the people benefitting from the dam approved of it overwhelmingly).

Capitalism clearly created contradictory attitudes in people, he said, but World War II had proved that large-scale cooperation could be obtained. Understanding, he felt, was the key to reconciling individualism and the competitive ideal with democratic planning. Citizens should be put in control of as many choices as possible; they did not have to know the technical processes to make the choices. Flexible planning, with as much local participation as possible, he said, was necessary; for Hicks regarded it as essential for the well-being of mankind: "By now it is quite clear that the problem of the re-integration of human personality is inseparable from the problem of the integration of society. If, that is, the individual could feel that social forces were under control, and in some real sense under *his* control, the new fears could be conquered" (240).

The small towns could be saved if three things were done: (1) if they were given some economic basis for existing (not necessarily self-sufficiency as in the nineteenth century); (2) if good living standards and "decent urban knowledge" about solving community problems could be provided; (3) and if activities could be fostered that brought the townspeople together in satisfying ways. Although he suggested that no single formula would redeem towns, a powerful person (such as a factory owner) could perhaps provide impetus. But paternalism could not do it alone: "The leader who counts is the one who can win followers, not buy them" (217).

In concluding, Hicks said that he had learned to moderate his

natural optimism of preserving the towns and of providing proper
leadership and that he was not sure the problems could be solved.
But he felt that since some solutions were possible for the immediate future, they were enough to worry about. He thought,
he said, of a fire commissioners' meeting that he was going to at-
tend later that day. It might be boring, the outcome might be
disappointing, but part of it would be informative, and he might
be able to do something. "As a matter of fact, I expect to enjoy
parts of the evening, as I have enjoyed parts—and rather large
parts—of the whole experience with which this book has dealt"
(276).

In 1957, Hicks quit participating in town affairs because he
became busy with his literary work and teaching—and partly
because he ran out of patience. His Roxborough seems like a very
discouraging place for a public-spirited person—intellectual or
no. Yet the book is his most original contribution to social
thought. Although he had studied what others had to say about
society and about small towns, he presented his own observations
with such veracity and as the result of so much of his thought and
experience—both with community affairs and with radical
politics—that *Small Town* is a clarifying, moving book.

VI *Later Comments on the Small Town*

Having become something of an "expert" on small towns, Hicks
was asked in later years to review books on the subject; and he
sometimes wrote and talked about it. In 1953, seven years after
Small Town was published, Hicks reviewed what had happened
in "Roxborough." Population had grown to 987 by 1950, people
were more prosperous, national politics commanded more attention than it formerly had, and more teachers and professional
people lived there. In many ways the town was becoming a
suburb, for more people were now commuting to work in factories and to white-collar jobs around Albany. The old-timers no
longer knew everyone in town, and a Democrat could be elected
in a nonpartisan effort. Catholics were more tolerated, but Jews,
Negroes, or immigrants would probably not be. "Except for purely physical conditions—space, fresh air, quiet (unless one lives on
the highway), woods to walk in, ground to plant, hills to look
at—all of which are important—life in Roxborough grows more
and more like life in the rest of the Capital District."[7]

Hicks did not object to some of the standardization of life in the town. Like Jacques Barzun in *God's Country and Mine*, he defended mass culture to some extent; for the American cultural mélange could satisfy a variety of tastes. Furthermore, the suburbanite did not have to conform slavishly to mass tastes and culture; and many people did not. When discussing in 1960 *This Demi-Paradise* by Margaret Halsey, a novel about the suburbs, Hicks said: "I think there are a lot more people like the Fitzgibbonses in the suburbs and in America than Helen's Measurers ever discover. [He was discussing characters in the novel.] They are not the noisy rebels against conformity; in fact, they don't think of themselves as rebels at all. They are merely people who want to be themselves and have discovered that, no matter where they live, they can be. If there is any hope for the future, it is in such people."[8]

By 1972 Hicks had resigned himself to a possible loss of the small town into the urban web. The small towns were not a guide to the future, Hicks said. Technological progress was heading for a crisis. "If it survives, it will absorb the Stoningtons, the Kents—and the Roosevelts. If not, it will take the small towns into the abyss. In the meantime, for many of us, the small town is a better place than most in which to spend whatever time remains."[9] (Hicks was referring to the time left for Western civilization, but he may have been thinking unconsciously of his own life.) Also in that year, Hicks argued in agreement with Vance Packard that America was a "nation of strangers" because the citizens moved around too much. Such rootlessness had more disadvantages than advantages, Hicks said, because of the problems in establishing and in keeping identity.[10]

Hicks showed himself to be a man concerned with and knowledgeable about how we live in American communities. His concerns may also turn out to have been prophetic, for the recent criticism of our wasteful ways and our fondness for big organization has grown on many fronts. Pollution, alienation, and problems related to bigness have in recent years seemed even more evil. One example of the protest is E. F. Schumacher's *Small Is Beautiful*, which has inspired a whole school of thought. Hicks's concern for what has happened to the small town and to the whole society because of the above problems is almost as important a part of his contribution as is his defense of the serious novel.

CHAPTER 7

Back to Criticism:
The 1940s and 1950s

GRADUALLY during the 1940s, after having adjusted to his disillusionment with Marxism, Hicks turned again to criticism. We noted in chapter 6 that he wrote occasional critical pieces during the early and middle 1940s while producing his novels and his study of small-town life, as well as busying himself with other enterprises. Then in 1949 he began contributing reviews to the *New Leader*, an anti-Communist liberal magazine conducted under the loving care of Sol Levitas. Printed on pulp paper in black ink—much like the format of the *Nation* and the *New Republic*—this weekly journal was a labor of love to its editors and contributors. The pay for Hicks's work was low, but it gave him a chance to be heard again. In November, 1951, he became its literary editor; but, when he soon realized that he could not function in that position and live in Grafton, he had himself labeled as literary consultant. The relationship prospered; and, on December 1, 1952, Hicks began his column "Living with Books," which appeared every other week. During Hicks's nine-year association with the *New Leader* (he wrote for other journals as well), he practiced his revised literary theories and his approach to reviewing, and he contributed fruitful criticism of novels.

I Literary Commentary of the Early 1940s

Although the early and mid-1940s were a time of intellectual convalescence for Hicks—especially from criticism—he did contribute several literary articles to the *American Mercury*, the *Antioch Review*, *College English*, the *English Journal*, the *New Republic*, and *Tomorrow*. A sampling of these works indicates his literary mood and his attempts to come to terms with literature on a nondoctrinaire basis.

In "Literature in This Global War" (1943), Hicks talked about a few World War II novels that had already appeared, including John Steinbeck's *The Moon Is Down*, Somerset Maugham's *The Hour Before Dawn*, Joseph Freeman's *Never Call Retreat*, Erskine Caldwell's *All Night Long*, Pearl Buck's *The Dragon Seed*, and Ira Wolfert's *Battle for the Solomons*. He offered only slight approval for the novels by Freeman and Wolfert, he praised Buck's and Steinbeck's novels, he blasted Caldwell's and Maugham's, and he concluded that the best books would be written after the war. Because he viewed the war as unromantic and mysterious, he observed that whether the postwar novelists would write "in bitterness or in hope depends rather on the character of the peace than on the nature of the war."[1]

A year later in "The Shape of Postwar Literature," Hicks suggested that the authors would not be like those after World War I who had expressed disillusionment and expatriotism. Writers would probably (he hoped) stick to sober philosophical thinking, abnormal psychology, and metaphysical concerns. Some protest novels, such as those of the 1930s, had recently been published; but, since that era was over, Hicks thought writers were likely to turn from the novel dealing with a specific problem to "questions for which there are no easy answers." Realism would become more flexible but remain realism. It would probably be a bad time for letters in general, Hicks concluded, but this difficulty might possibly enable a few writers to rise to greatness.[2]

When Hicks reviewed Alfred Kazin's *On Native Grounds*, he defended himself against Kazin's attack on his radicalism of the 1930s, but he partly agreed with Kazin's criticisms. Although he and others in the 1930s were wrong in many ways, Hicks said, they were right in believing that writers could not ignore the world. He pointed out that both he and Kazin felt ours was "a sick literature of a sick society."[3]

In a 1946 review of three novels for *American Mercury*, Hicks indicates his treatment of fiction in this post-Marxist time. James Farrell's novel *Bernard Clare*, Hicks wrote, covered too much detail about Clare's young life. (He was another Danny O'Neill, Hicks said.) But Farrell was honest, which gave him his success: "His working faith has only two articles: the importance of James

T. Farrell and the importance of honest writing. It has carried him no inconsiderable distance." Although Howard Fast in *The American* had shown honesty and an open expression of his simplistic communism, Hicks observed that Fast was too prone to see his hero John Peter Altgeld as all good and pure—although Hicks admitted the character is given more than one dimension. Whether the people's politicians are demagogues or prophets is "a complicated matter, and Fast, who must have his heroes, wants to keep things simple and clear." Hicks did not approve of this simplicity.

The most important novel that Hicks reviewed in this 1946 article was Robert Penn Warren's *All the King's Men*, which Hicks asserted was a better book about Huey Long than John Dos Passos's *Number One*. Jack Burden, he said, was the perfect spokesman for Warren, and his quest for meaning was the appropriate theme. To Hicks, this novel presented the problem of the political boss who was corrupt but who got things done; Warren, however, did not suggest what needed to be done to change the obviously bad system, as Lincoln Steffens and George Bernard Shaw had done. The character Burden ultimately rejected the idea that life was a cosmic accident, a Big Twitch; but what its meaning was he did not say. Warren had learned, Hicks said, that the social problem could not stand by itself, and he had tackled it along with the moral and philosophical problems. Each reader had to make of it what he chose. Hicks talked about the style of this novel more than he usually did, although he presented no formalistic analysis. Warren had given the protagonist-narrator "a colloquial and yet sophisticated style that is wholly appropriate to Jack Burden and beautifully suited to the purposes of the novel." Warren kept to common speech, but "his prose rises when necessary into brilliant but unforced imagery. . . . It is a prose that is never mannered and yet never lapses into stylelessness." The novel was skillfully fashioned and broad in scope; it was such a good book that it put Warren "in the very front rank of American novelists."[4]

As these reviews indicate, Hicks was a less fervent advocate of political certitude in the novel than he had been; and he suggested that novels should be of a metaphysical and philosophical kind rather than problem novels of simple protest. He was, in general, less polemical than in the 1930s; but he had not lost his

interest in or awareness of social problems, as we will see. Hicks
no longer considered himself an important critic who was carry-
ing the burden of social revolution through literary activity. He
had become a sensible and modest reviewer of books instead of a
self-styled cultural high priest.

II   *The Condition of Criticism in the 1950s*

When he returned to active reviewing, Hicks expressed his
dismay at the state of literary criticism and book reviewing. The
new criticism and academic formalism in general were often his
targets, but he also modified some of his views and found some of
his old critical heroes at fault—especially Van Wyck Brooks.
Upon assuming the title of literary editor of the *New Leader* in
1951, Hicks defended the importance of book reviewing, especially of the reviews written by lovers of books who showed
understanding of the writer. Such responsible reviewers—who
were rare among the many incompetent or "catty" critics—often
helped writers to see their problems; and, in the process, they
might help make literary history. Although few reviews influenced sales, except for a handful published in New York, books
were reviewed all over the nation in strange places and often with
discouraging results. Because the *New Leader* reviewers had
usually been book lovers, Hicks was glad to be associated with it.[5]

Indeed, the academic and dogmatic critics were often "The
Enemies of Literature," he asserted a year later. Much of the new
criticism was not only very bad but also bad for literature. He
used D. S. Savage's *The Withered Branch* as an example of bad
dogmatic criticism. To Hicks, a good critic was first a good reader
who would criticize a book if it needed it but who was "on the
writers' side, not with the enemies of literatures."[6] Hicks, who
was in favor of a personal kind of criticism, was not opposed to the
use of biographical facts about the author—an approach which
ran contrary to the new criticism. He dealt harshly, for example,
with R. W. Stallman's volume on Stephen Crane. Stallman's comments in the edition, Hicks asserted, "exemplify the 'new'
criticism in its most pedantic form, with much solemn discussion
of symbolism and a great parade of literary names." As a result,
Stallman added nothing to the study of Crane.

In the same 1952 review, on the other hand, Hicks praised

Katherine Ann Porter's book that discussed five influential writers. "Much of Miss Porter's criticism would horrify Mr. Stallman, because it is frankly biographical and that is for him the great heresy. Her essays make it clear how ridiculous his dogma is. No one can keep a sharper eye on the work of art, but she realizes that sometimes the art can be usefully approached by way of the artist, and, in any case, she is naturally interested in artists."[7] This review represents the kind of comment Hicks has often made about academic formalist criticism and scholarship. He expressed here an opinion he has continued to hold. From time to time, however, he did find certain formalist ideas useful.

Not only academic but also journalistic criticism came under fire from Hicks during the 1950s. In a column entitled "The State of Literary Journalism: Is The Serious Novel Expendable?" (1956), Hicks attacked Anthony West and other reviewers in the *New Yorker* for simply not doing their jobs and for being unfair snobs. The main problem was that there was "so little responsible literary journalism, so little serious reviewing, especially of fiction." By "serious" he did not mean highbrow, Hicks said; ". . . it is enough if the reviewer, having certain elementary qualifications, has read the book carefully, has thought about it, and has taken the trouble to state his thoughts clearly." To Hicks, the critics, as opposed to reviewers, were not paying enough attention to the contemporary novel; he cited Edmund Wilson, who asserted that he read only the classics, and Yvor Winters, who said that he could take a little of Joyce and Woolf but not any of Hemingway and Faulkner. Hicks concluded that such men were "no longer with us."[8]

Van Wyck Brooks also distressed Hicks because of his insistence that writers express affirmation and social idealism—an attitude which Hicks had already criticized, in 1944, in both Brooks and Bernard DeVoto. Writers who repudiated the masses were not necessarily bad, Hicks said, as Brooks had insisted and as DeVoto had argued in *The Literary Fallacy*. To Hicks, Mark Twain had been against the masses, but he and other writers could not help their feelings. Books should be taken for what they are, not what the critic thought they should have been, for writers have "to make what they can of their wanderings, and we are foolish if we let our impatience keep us from discovering and enjoying and profiting from what they made." They write about people as they see them, he said. "I too have sometimes erred in refusing to take literature as it is, but I have sworn to do better in the future."[9]

In 1952, Hicks again disagreed with Brooks; for he thought that Joyce, Lawrence, Proust, Stein, and Pound had not forsaken "the joy of life and humane tradition" as Brooks had asserted in *The Confident Years*. Hicks admitted that he admired Brooks for his idealism and his affirmativeness but said that he was distressed that Brooks could find so little to admire in writers whose world view differed from his, that is, who raised doubts about humanity. "Joyce, Proust, Lawrence, Hemingway, Faulkner, and Eliot are our great writers, and if they arouse in Brooks nothing but peevish dismay, so much the worse for him." Jeffersonian optimism about the possibility of human progress like that of Brooks had to be proven and needed to be put to the test. Such ideals, Hicks argued, needed to be criticized and strengthened.[10]

A year later Hicks again found Brooks's views in *The Writer in America* wrongheaded and alienated from the good writers, and he also argued, contrary to Brooks, that the formalist critic Allen Tate (although too fond of the oblique in *The Forlorn Demon*) was "making an honorable contribution to critical discussion in our time." The fault in Brooks lay with much liberal thought, which demanded affirmation, Hicks said, and such thought would be a calamity today. "Even Lewis Mumford, whom Brooks singles out for praise, sees that the crisis of modern civilization is a real crisis, not to be exorcised by cheerful words." Writers, Hicks said, had to write honestly and effectively about how they felt.[11]

Another critic who came under scrutiny was Edmund Wilson; Hicks characterized him as cold-hearted but brilliant. When Hicks launched his "Living with Books" column in 1952 and reviewed Wilson's *The Shores of Light*, he opined that Wilson "hits the bull's eye more regularly than anybody else." Wilson had first recognized the importance of Ring Lardner and had defended Thornton Wilder during the radical 1930s—and had been right. He had also advocated taking communism away from Communists and had seen by 1934 that no one could take it away from the Stalinists. Hicks found *The Shores of Light* an improvement for Wilson: "He has always displayed a warm feeling toward books, but in these essays there is a warm feeling toward human beings—the only important quality, I think, in which his work in general is deficient."[12]

Thus, by the early 1950s, Hicks had formulated a new set of attitudes toward criticism and critics. He was determined to be the right kind of critic himself and to come to the defense of serious literature of all types and with different political and socio-economic views.

III   *On the Nature of the Novel*

The literary form Hicks wanted most to defend was the novel. During this period he devoted much of his writing to defining its primary task, to dealing with kinds of novels (such as social and psychological), and to arguing for the value and the durability of fiction, since some writers said the novel was dying. After World War II, novels dealt with "psychological and moral conflicts," Hicks said in 1948: ". . . the focus of inquiry has altered . . . the empahsis now falls on what is inside man rather than on what is outside," such as the social concerns of the 1920s and 1930s. Robert Penn Warren, for example, in *All the King's Men*, was interested in the political and social struggles of Huey Long's Louisiana "as expressions of psychological and moral conflicts."[13]

To Hicks, the basic requirement of the novel was to present "life." For example, in "The Best American Novels since 1945" (1953), he said, "And that, after all, is what we have a right to ask of fiction—that it should waken in us a sense of life." After listing some of the current novels, he concluded that "the years since the war have not been sterile."[14] And again in 1955, when discussing the realistic novel *The Young Lovers*, by Julian Halevy, he said, "I look back on the book with special affection. It is about people I liked, having experiences that I can believe in and share. . . . But the reader feels that here is life, and, as E. M. Forster has said, that is what counts in the novel."

The realistic novel was still vital to Hicks, but he also thought that ". . . a preference for one kind of fiction ought not to blind a reader to the merits of other kinds."[15] In 1956 he defined the truly serious fiction: "What the serious novelist does, through some combination of will and insight and craftsmanship, is to transform experience in such a way as to give it meaning. We live in a world that . . . is rich in experience, so rich that for most of us everything is blurred. The desperation Saul Bellow describes in *Seize the Day*, the desperation of the blind alley, is an experience that millions of men and women have had without learning anything from it; the meaning is what Bellow has known how not only to discover but also to communicate."[16]

IV   *The Social Novel*

Although, as we have noted, Hicks had changed his attitude about novels with social themes from his position in the 1930s, he still expressed an interest in them. Hicks said in 1951, for instance, that in the 1930s radical critics had expected too much from "social realism." But, he asserted, "I cannot accept the contemporary dogma [of certain critics] that would ban social realism altogether. I grant that other approaches are valid, but it still seems to me that one way of getting at human beings is to see them in relation to the social organization of which they are a part."[17]

A year later, Hicks expressed a distinction between novels of social protest and those of social criticism. The protest novel was aimed at a specific evil—slavery, the Chicago stockyards, the sufferings of migrant Okies. "The novel of social criticism is concerned in a larger way with the social structure. It is broader and deeper, and if its influence is harder to measure, its life is usually longer." Protest novels had only historical interest, but novels of criticism had been a "mighty force in our literature." To Hicks, social criticism was waning; writers like Faulkner, Fitzgerald, and Hemingway were not studied for the elements of social criticism in them by "the molders of literary opinion." Since the 1930s, writers had reacted against the idea of one solution to all problems; they now saw that solving social problems was "a never-ending job." Writers were turning to the novel of the "human condition," which could lead to artificiality and abstractness.

Meanwhile, social novelists such as John Dos Passos, John P. Marquand, James Gould Cozzens, and Herman Wouk had turned conservative; and writers like Cozzens showed no passion in their fiction. "We have no clear evidence that conservatism can provide a basis for the postwar literary renaissance that is so long overdue," because society was changing too rapidly for the conservative mind, and sensitive writers would continue to feel "a sense of estrangement." "Good novels," Hicks concluded, "can and will be written about the American scene, and I believe that most of them will belong in the tradition of social criticism."[18]

Again in 1953 Hicks expressed his persistent interest in social novels. When writing about the novels by John Phillips, Oakley Hall, and Allan Seager, he found it ". . . gratifying, these days, to find three talented authors willing to take a good look at the contemporary American scene instead of disporting themselves in private worlds."[19] In 1954 Hicks defended Harriette Arnow's novel *The Dollmaker*. To Hicks, some highbrow critics would probably not like it, thinking that it was too folksy—since it was about a Kentucky woman in a Detroit housing project—and was merely sociological. Such a view would be a mistake: "It does, to be sure, present a sociological phenomenon, and it presents it so vividly that the reader is bound to think seriously about the quality of life in America. But that is only a secondary achievement; Mrs. Arnow's great achievement is to have recorded so truly, with all its misery and all its grandeur, the ordeal of the human spirit."[20]

Hicks even expressed the hope in 1955 that the social novel might be coming back—minus the mistakes that had plagued it in the 1930s. The "new" novelists after the 1930s had shied away from "the larger issues of contemporary life," but many new novels were good, such as Jean Stafford's *The Catherine Wheel*. "And yet to some of us it has seemed unhealthy that there should be large and important areas of American experience about which so many talented young writers felt that they could not write." The trend away from social novels may have reversed in 1955, he suggested, but he cautioned that we did not want "a revival of the propaganda novel that flourished in the 30's." To Hicks, Ring Lardner, Jr.'s *The Ecstasy of Owen Muir* was just such a book, for it was "sounding the clarion call against . . . fascism. This is not merely a novel with a message; it is an anachronism." Budd Schulberg's *On the Waterfront* was a good muckraking novel about union racketeering, but Norman Mailer's *The Deer Park* tried to be a propaganda novel. "By and large, however, Mailer's anger and disgust are so diffused that one cannot classify him as a propagandist" and his book was a failure.

Hicks went on in the same article to deal with questions of form in social novels. The novels of protest in the 1930s talked of problems but not about the "people in whose lives the problems have their reality." On the other hand, the "new" novelists wrote as if social problems did not exist. There was no danger of writers repeating the errors of the 1930s, Hicks said, since the political situation was different. Dogmatism had been in the air then, and writers were grouped under the Marxist banner. Today they were not grouped: "Most of them simply recognize that, of all human problems, the problems of society are not the least important." The lessons of craftsmanship would not be forgotten; the new emphasis on "form, texture, symbolism, imagery, and all the rest of it took extravagant forms, but in itself was good." But writers now knew that "one doesn't have to cease to be a craftsman in order to write about social issues." In fact, social themes made for diversity in literature, and to be concerned with them could be "a sign of a return to the intellectual community of self-confidence and hope."[21]

In 1956 Hicks expressed a solution to the problem of politics in fiction. Although a novel could show certain political attitudes, it had to create a fictional world of its own if it were going to last. He defended Graham Greene's *The Quiet American* as a novel with an immediate political opinion and a long-term value, for some critics had said that, because it was anti-American, it was a bad novel. Hicks said that a literary journalist might have to talk about the immediate political issues in a novel but that a literary *critic* looked at it in the largest possible perspective. Thus, the better, more responsible reviewer had to judge a political novel on more than one level; he could not let immediate issues blind him completely to the qualities that might make the book last. Sound or unsound ideas did not necessarily make or break a novel. On the other hand, a political novel was a political act and had to be judged in light of the political moment as well.[22]

This statement and another Hicks made in 1957 indicated that he had come to terms with the problem of politics and social issues in fiction, a process he had been going through since the 1940s, as we have noted. Reviewing Irving Howe's *Politics and the Novel*, in which Howe argued that ideology was of central importance, Hicks asserted that even in a political novel moral issues were more basic than political ideology. Certain fine novels did fit Howe's thesis that ideology must play a dominant role, but Hicks thought that "ideology may be less important even in these novels than he supposes," for the novel comes sooner or later to a moral issue: "In the successful novel, the moral issue is never raised in an abstract fashion and is never solved in terms of the absolutely right or the absolutely wrong, even though the novelist may himself be absolutist."

After Hicks had quoted Howe's statement that a writer often allowed opposition in his fiction against his own wishes, Hicks stated that "This is the spirit in which the great novelist approaches all moral issues, whether or not politics is involved." Novels such as John Dos Passos's *U.S.A.*, Robert Penn Warren's *All the King's Men*, and Lionel Trilling's *The Middle of the Journey* "in their more important aspects" raised questions about the "morality of power and the morality of opposition." The loss of a specific political ideology by a political novelist need not be a problem, Hicks insisted; such a writer could work in the "fundamental tradition of the great political novels" (meaning the ones that raised basic moral issues).[23] Hicks thus managed to evade the quagmire of political ideology with its stultifying, absolutist effect on a writer (the way it had affected him in the 1930s). From this point of view, Hicks continued thereafter to deal with social issues in fiction.

V   *The Future of the Novel*

If the novel had been dying, as many suggested, all of Hicks's theorizing might have been meaningless; but he insisted throughout this period—and indeed continued to insist—that the novel was alive and well. In 1951, for example, Hicks wrote an essay called "The Novel Isn't Dying" in which he mentioned new novels by James Jones, J. D. Salinger, Herman Wouk, and William Styron. He admitted that 1951 was not like any year in the 1920s, when many important books had been published. We were not seeing a renaissance. "But we have technical skill (of a very high order); we have seriousness; we have power. I not only see no signs that the novel is dying; I have the strongest hunch that it is about to display a new vitality."[24]

Hicks was still presenting the same argument in 1957 when he edited *The Living Novel*, a collection of essays, and wrote for it his "Afterword: The Enemies of the Novel" in which he argued that the novel was not expendable in American life; for it gave readers an understanding of the changes and anxieties of their time. The novelist paid attention to life and made the reader see small segments of life more clearly; he also increased the reader's capacity for experience. We had many good writers—whether they were geniuses or not—and the novel was in safe hands. Among the enemies of the novel, he said, were those who lamented that we now had no geniuses. The other enemies he listed were the distractions that made ours an age of inattention, the cleavage between the popular and the serious novel, the middlebrows who wanted the novel to "stop being serious while continuing to seem serious," the highbrows who did not like modern novels because they were hard to classify, and the incompetent book reviewers. Mass culture and mass communication were not enemies; for, though mass culture was indifferent to the serious novel, it had "by-products of great value." To Hicks, we needed to enlarge the audience for novels instead of attacking the mass media.[25]

VI   Hicks's Critical Method and Theories

A few other ideas need to be mentioned in order to characterize Hicks's theory and practice during this period, the 1950s. Besides coming to grips with the social issues in literature mentioned above, Hicks evolved a set of ideas and a method of reviewing that made him an informative, interesting critic. Often he would respond personally (although not emotionally) to the ideas he saw in a book, and he would discuss them. At the same time he always made clear to the reader what the book was about or what it said; he did not turn the review into his own ideological tract. Furthermore, he was always as charitable as he could be, even though he did not hesitate to indicate shortcomings; he related a lot of the story but did not give away the ending if he felt that was crucial; and he was very good at analyzing the themes of the books. When the reader finished Hicks's review, he knew what the book was about and was stimulated to read it with perhaps more insight than he would have had without the information Hicks had presented.

A typical comment on a novel Hicks saw as faulty but with some merit is his review of Dannie Abse's *Some Corner of an English Field*: "Mr. Abse tells the story in a rather offhand fashion, so that it takes some time for the reader to discover where he is going, and he devotes more attention to minor characters than seems necessary. By comparison with many of his contemporaries . . . he strikes me as an inept novelist. But here . . . he creates an atmosphere, and here he has brought to life a complex character." In both this book and in Abse's *Ash on a Young Man's Sleeve*, Hicks wrote that the reader felt "an essential honesty, a determination not to be betrayed into falseness by the desire to achieve certain literary effects. Abse has his own way of looking at things, and, whatever his shortcomings as a novelist, he knows how to make us see what he sees."[26]

In the case of Frederick Buechner's novel *The Return of Ansel Gibbs*, Hicks felt the novel did not create the illusion that Gibbs was a man who could bear large responsibilities; but this view did not affect Hicks's enjoyment of the novel. The characters were real in "ways that are important to me," although they were also unreal in others; and Buechner had "a fine sense of the complexity of human motives."[27]

If he found a novel to be very bad, Hicks said so. Reviewing Henrietta Buckmaster's anti-fascist novel *Bread from Heaven*, for instance, Hicks said it was a bad novel which turned a noble idea "into mush." Ideas were made simplistic: fascism equaled evil; the death force was opposed to the life force. "It is the kind of book," Hicks said, "that has given the novel of social problems its present low reputation."[28] In this manner Hicks would proceed by giving the writer as much encouragement and credit as he could; but he did not hesitate to indicate the faults he saw, to discuss the ideas in a book when appropriate, and to identify and clarify themes.

Hicks dealt with matters of style and form when they were important, but he was usually necessarily brief. Occasionally he would mention the diction or a figure of speech that he found striking. George Anthony Weller's novel *The Crack in the Column*, for example, has a passage that reads, ". . . so Greece has not cooked well? The mush of beans and water, without bread, has been burned too much for Slav taste, has it?" After Hicks quoted the passage from the novel (which is about Greek Communists fighting and losing after World War II German occupation), he commented, "Would it not be difficult to say how many kinds of awareness have gone into this passage, with its extended and beautifully sustained metaphor?"[29] Seldom did Hicks use his limited space to quote passages in his reviews, and even less often did he discuss style in such specific terms. But, when he did so, his reviews were better.

More often his comments on style were brief, general, but usually accurate. Of Shirley Ann Grau's collection of short stories, for example, Hicks said her style was "direct, firm, idiomatic" and that her dialogue had "an air of perfect, unobtrusive authenticity. And here and there a single, sharp descriptive phrase lights up the scene."[30] Another example of his treatment of form is his unfavorable comparison of John Steinbeck's *East of Eden* with Gerald Sykes's *The Center of the Stage*. Steinbeck's novel was too formless, he said, and inconsistent in point of view and technique. The character Cathy was an unbelievable monster, and the Cain-Abel theme was handled awkwardly. The Sykes novel, on the other hand, was more precise and controlled; and the main evil character, Carlotta, was believable. Hicks said that Steinbeck's novel would be more popular but that he thought the other novel would be "more rewarding" to readers.[31]

Also, from time to time, Hicks offered theories on style and technique in general. Reviewing Mark Schorer's novel, *The Wars of Love*, he attempted to define technique and content. Schorer had said in an earlier essay that "The difference between content, or experience, and achieved content, or art, is technique." His novel showed that content as well as method made it good, Hicks said, even through Schorer did display technical skill. Yet it was "the quality of its insights, not the technique," that made the reader understand the novel. The difference between insight and technique might be unimportant as Schorer defined them, Hicks said. Perhaps, however, the problem could be seen more sharply if this novel were compared with some other which had technical skill but was tepid because it treated only the surface. When Hicks mentioned other novels that he was reviewing, he suggested that they were perhaps poor because they lacked technical discipline. "That is the point at issue. There is, as Mr. Schorer says, a great difference between content and achieved content, between experience and art, but I am not satisfied that the intervening process can be adequately summed up with the word 'technique.' "[32]

Hicks also expressed a theory when discussing James Gould Cozzens that goes back at least to Samuel Taylor Coleridge and has been mentioned by Lionel Trilling and others—the theory of "reconciling opposites." The earlier novels of Cozzens were good, but they did not have a quality exhibited in his 1957 novel, *By Love Possessed*; "He was good, a fine craftsman, conscientious, honest, shrewd, even wise. But I could discover in his books little evidence of the kind of inner pressure that is essential to greatness. He was too detached, I felt, too uncommitted, to be a

great creative artist. That earlier judgment is now called in question . . . by the new novel." Cozzens was committed in this
novel; the "inner tension" was there; and the book, Hicks admitted, "moves me as I have been moved by no other book of
his."[33] This notion of tension or inner pressure in a literary work is
a formalist theory which Hicks had accepted somewhere along
the way, consciously or unconsciously. So was his differentiation
between content and technique. By and large, however, Hicks
did not venture far into theory; instead, he discussed each novel
on its merits and enunciated whatever theory he felt was relevant
to reviewing that particular book.

VII *Some Comments on Specific Authors*

The best way to show how Hicks worked is to explore further
his statements about specific authors. Some of his views during
this period have been mentioned—for example, concerning
Cozzens, Steinbeck, Penn Warren, Trilling, Greene, Arnow,
Stafford, Schulberg, Bellow; his comments about other authors
indicate the versatility and usefulness of his criticism.

John Dos Passos, Hicks said in 1949, was a novelist he had been
partly wrong about during the 1930s. He still admired Dos Passos
as an honest observer, but Hicks felt that he had been overen-
thusiastic about Dos Passos's radicalism and had failed to see the
sense of futility which was expressed even in the trilogy *U. S. A.*
Hicks had failed as a radical critic, he confessed, to notice that
Dos Passos wrote little about proletarians. His radical heroine
Mary French was ineffectual, and her onetime lover was an op-
portunistic radical. A closer look might have shown the essential
skepticism evident in Dos Passos's work—minus perhaps any saving faith, such as that later found in William Faulkner and even
Ernest Hemingway. But Hicks argued that he had been right
about Dos Passos's concern for industrial life and his bold confrontation with modern society. So Hicks came to terms with Dos
Passos, who had moved toward the right politically; Hicks also
adjusted the critical mistakes he had made in the 1930s. Perhaps
no one has explained Dos Passos any better and treated him more
fairly. Although the best explanation offered of Dos Passos in recent years has been that he was writing tragic satire, Hicks leaves
room in his evaluation for that idea.[34]

When John P. Marquand came under the Hicks scrutiny in an

informative essay he wrote in 1950, Hicks indicated that Marquand's epistolary novel *The Late George Apley* had misled his readers into thinking that he was primarily a satirist. By and large, he did not satirize the upper-class people he wrote about, Hicks said, because he did not have a set standard from which to view or judge the upper-class world. Marquand was aware of class distinctions, but he was more subtle than that. His novels presented neither great ecstacy nor tragedy; instead, they contained a view of people who were accepting things—knowing that they were not angels in heaven but recognizing also they could be worse ("the doctrine of the half loaf"). Marquand dealt with domestic things—with careers and marriage up and down the upper part of the social scale. He wrote, Hicks said, in an easy, good style (Hicks cited the beginning of *B. F.'s Daughter* as an example) and dealt with a world of rules, a world in which there were "few spectacular tragedies and a good deal of quiet desperation."[35]

William Faulkner, whom Hicks had attacked during the 1930s, was the subject of several articles during the 1940s and 1950s. As early as 1946, Hicks had talked of Faulkner's importance in an article about psychoneurotic (P-N) fiction. Faulkner did not deal with abnormal minds merely to shock but to show social decay. Faulkner portrayed the characters he did, Hicks said, because of "his vision of the disintegration of a culture" and because he saw "in the maladjustments of individuals a kind of significance that lies outside the range of the professional psychologist."[36]

Two articles Hicks wrote in 1951 indicate his interest in Faulkner. "Some Literary Detective Work" listed the changes and inconsistencies in the names of characters and in their personalities in various stories. Faulkner sometimes forgot to keep the characters straight, but he often changed them on purpose to suit his artistic needs, Hicks said. Looking closely at the changes could help the reader understand "Faulkner's ways of creating truth and dream."[37] That same year Hicks discussed in "Faulkner's South, A Northern Interpretation," Faulkner's attitudes toward the South. He concluded that Faulkner was anti-industrial and lamented the passing of agrarian ways.[38]

A year later, reviewing Irving Howe's study of Faulkner, Hicks agreed with Howe that Faulkner had many attitudes toward the South and that he was shaping a new myth: ". . . man falls, not from the grace of an ordered aristocratic society, but from the innocence of harmonious relationship with nature." But Howe did not fully explore this myth, Hicks said: "Exploitation, of either man or nature, is the root of all evil in the new myth." To Hicks, "exploitation of the Negroes [was] only one of many forms."[39] This interesting view of Faulkner is nicely stated and presents the kind of insight that often got lost in all the formalist studies of Faulkner.

In 1957 Hicks suggested that Faulkner had written a good novel in *The Town* but one not nearly as good as *The Hamlet*. Hicks also said that in other recent stories—*Knight's Gambit*, *Requiem for a Nun*, *A Fable*, and *Big Woods*—Faulkner had used his skill to conceal an absence of insight: "It is as if this wonderful rhetoric, which he so boldly fashioned to serve his purposes, had taken over and was plunging ahead like a runaway locomotive." Perhaps, Hicks suggested, Faulkner had been distracted by having become a public figure in the 1950s.[40] Hicks showed once again his ability to discuss an important writer in a balanced, informed way. Although he was not as original a Faulkner critic as Malcolm Cowley and others, his comments did not add to the obfuscation offered by the countless formalist studies of Faulkner.

When Eudora Welty came under scrutiny from Hicks in a 1952 article, he defended her as more than a regionalist and a purveyor of bizarre violence. She was not interested in violence for its own sake, he said, but in its effect on people. Welty could be very factual but could easily slip into the subjective: "So far as technique is concerned, her characteristic quality is just this perfect balance between the objective and the subjective." She had two persistent themes. The first of these was the mystery of personality, which took two forms, the mystery of others and the mystery of self. "The failure of human beings to understand one another, one of the perennial themes of literature, she treats often as tragedy and sometimes . . . as comedy." The second Welty theme was "the problem of what brings people together and what holds them apart." As an example of separateness, Hicks mentioned the story "Death of a Traveling Salesman."

Delta Wedding showed what Welty could do in the novel, Hicks said; she had achieved a "technical triumph" in the "constant, subtle shifting of point of view to render the most that can be rendered." The story was built around the mystery, he said, of the behavior of Uncle George Fairchild. Hicks cited *The Golden Apples* as a story that showed how Welty could make a story take on "the purity and . . . the universality of legend."

When Hicks defended Welty against such critics as Diana Trilling, Margaret Marshall, and Isaac Rosenfeld, who felt that Welty was too regional and that she wrote about people not worth writing about, Hicks indicated her universality: "But if she shares in the heritage of the South, she also shares in the literary tradition of Western civilization, and shares it at least as fully and deeply as the most up-to-date New York intellectual. And not only that: she proves, as the good regionalists have always proved, that the deeper one goes into the heart of a region, the more one transcends its geographical boundaries."[41]

John Steinbeck got a tolerant nod from Hicks in 1954 with *Sweet Thursday* because the novel was light and fun and "as shamelessly sentimental as . . . *Cannery Row*, but there are many amusing scenes." In *East of Eden*, Steinbeck had written a serious novel which was in part very bad. "By comparison, this extravaganza [*Sweet Thursday*] is a joy. It does, however, raise some perplexing questions about John Steinbeck. He exhibits here, as he has exhibited again and again in the past twenty-five years, many of the talents of a first-rate novelist, and yet it has been a long time since he wrote anything that could be called a first-rate novel. The more serious he is, the clearer his limitations become, and it is only in such an irresponsible farce as *Sweet Thursday* that he seems to do what he wants to do."[42]

C. P. Snow always got favorable reviews from Hicks. His novel *The New Men* was good, Hicks said, both as part of a series of novels and as an individual work. Although Hicks observed that Snow dealt with social issues of our time in England, he felt that the Britisher was more concerned with psychological effects than sociological ones. Hicks agreed to some extent with Frank O'Connor that Snow was more like Trollope than Joyce: "It is true that Snow, who is up-to-date in content, is in some ways old-fashioned in manner. . . . It may be that he is not, as O'Connor suggests, fighting a rearguard action; he may be pointing out a path, albeit a difficult path, to the future."[43]

Nelson Algren seemed to Hicks to be a good craftsman and also a better novelist than John Steinbeck because he was not sentimental; for, to Hicks, an overly sentimental attitude toward humans was erroneous. *A Walk on the Wild Side*, Hicks said in 1956, showed that Algren had "grown steadily in craftsmanship, so that he has become one of our more resourceful writers of fiction." By writing about disreputable people, Algren developed the Whitman themes that such people were a part of us all and were made into greater humans by their suffering and their having been lost than were those individuals who had never had such experiences. To Hicks, "Such an attitude might easily lead a writer into sentimentality, but Algren has always avoided this trap. His prostitutes and vagrants are not romanticized as are the characters in *Cannery Row* and *Sweet Thursday*, nor does one ever feel about him, as one often feels about Steinbeck, that his admiration for his raffish characters is a literary pose." Algren did not force the reader's sympathy; he left him free to condemn the characters: "What he will not let the reader do is comfort himself with the belief that these people are non-human. Their humanity is insisted upon, and insisted upon successfully, because it is so apparent to Algren himself."[44]

James Jones got a different treatment. Although Hicks had found some value in *From Here to Eternity*, he argued that *Some Came Running* was a horrible novel. He called it a "painfully dull book," and the pain was "greatly exacerbated by the badness of the writing. . . . This is not just inept or careless writing; it is an assault upon the language." He quoted from the novel to illustrate the bad writing, and he attacked Jones for his idea that he was a born writer and that all he had to do was record information without artistry. To Hicks, "This naively romantic concept of the creative person and the creative process makes Jones an uncurable amateur. As an editor and a teacher of writing, I encounter many such amateurs, young men and women who have convinced themselves, somehow or other, that the finger of destiny is pointing straight at them." Most such people, Hicks said, were lazy and got discouraged, but not Jones, who had the success and luck of *From Here to Eternity*.

"Convinced that he is 'a writer by personality,' he believes that all he has to do is put words on paper and that if he agonizes enough in the process the result is bound to be good." Jones knew better, Hicks said, but held to a "theoretical primitivism" and also thought he was tough. Jones not only had written badly but also had held to the mistaken idea that all he had to do was put down on paper as many things as possible. "Because he is, in his intentions though only in his intentions, a serious writer, the lesson is made quite clear," Hicks concluded, "that there is no substitute for the disciplined imagination."[45]

Hicks became, then, a wide-ranging critic, especially of recent fiction. As we have observed heretofore, he was receptive and tolerant of different kinds of writing on different kinds of subjects. He also could wield an ax when he felt it was necessary, and, since he thought that James Jones needed the ax, he wielded it. He reviewed other kinds of books besides fiction, of course, and treated all of them with the same care. He was always an informative critic in the highest sense, for he brought to his reviewing a well-stocked and sensitive mind. His reader knew what was in a book when he finished a review by Hicks, and he also knew whether he wanted to read it.

On March 24, 1958, Hicks published his last column in the *New Leader*. He was grateful, he said, for having been allowed to review more than two hundred books of his own choosing. The publication of the magazine was a credit to those devoted to it, for it performed "an invaluable function." Hicks did not, however, cease reviewing books; for he began to contribute in this same year a regular column to the *Saturday Review*.

CHAPTER 8

Saturday Review *and After,*
1958–1977

A S we have noted, in the winter of 1958 Hicks was hired to
write a book column for the *Saturday Review*, and his first
column "Literary Horizons" appeared on April 5, 1958. Since
Hicks had pretty well established his critical practices, his *Saturday Review* articles were similar to the previous ones in the *New
Leader*. He remained essentially the same critic in the years
1958–1969, in other words, that he had been in the early 1950s.
He did continue, however, to grow in power and perception and
to refine his work. As a result, this late period was the apex of his
career after many years of struggle and relative obscurity; and his
comments on literature during the *Saturday Review* years are
rewarding and interesting to read, as are the essays and the
reviews that he wrote after his retirement from that publication
on May 24, 1969. He continued to study the new trends in fiction,
to refine his theory and critical practice, and to write valuable
and engaging essays about scores of writers, both old and new. He
also had some harsh words to say about a few authors, but most
notably about Norman Mailer.

I   *Trends in the Novel*

While keeping his eye on specific novelists, Hicks made
general comments of interest about trends in recent decades.
Late in 1959, for example, he wrote "The Quest in a Quiet
Time" to defend the fiction of the 1950s. He agreed with Norman Mailer that the decade was one in which the writer did not
know who the alienating enemy was. But most writers had continued writing, as had Saul Bellow, Wright Morris, Carson McCullers, Flannery O'Connor, and J. D. Salinger. Their lit-

erature was for many critics "too quiet, too lacking in boldness"; but Hicks liked it: ". . . to me there is something reassuring in the quietness with which so many of the writers of this period carry on their work. I like it better than the noisiness of Mailer and the Beatniks. . . . The writers who look steadily and thoughtfully and imaginatively at the human condition have something to say to us now, and I believe that some of them will be saying more as time goes on."[1]

In "As Fiction Faces the Sixties," Hicks admitted that much popular fiction would be written to please the same people of our mass culture who were entertained by television; but some good serious fiction would be published; indeed, he asserted, "That serious fiction should be kept alive in the sixties is, I hope I do not need to say, important. To put the argument in its simplest terms, here is one of the media for the expression of deep sensibility, free imagination, and the critical temper. Here is the antithesis of the gadget, the gag, and the fix."[2] A change in emphasis had occurred in fiction, and Hicks liked it. Writers since World War II did not, by and large, have a program to improve society and were not particularly alienated from it. He observed in "On the Threshold of the Enduring" in 1964 that, since society was changing so rapidly, novelists could not keep up with journalism; as a result, novelists sought ways for the individual to do better in life. "Out of this search . . . they have created fiction that is of the greatest possible contemporary relevance and may be of enduring importance."[3]

Another clarifying essay on the novel in the 1960s was his column entitled "Signatures to the Significance of the Self" of 1964, in which he talked of the nonprotest writers, the ones who took society for granted and explored problems of the self. He listed among these John P. Marquand, John O'Hara, James Gould Cozzens, Herbert Gold, and J. D. Salinger. He mentioned Bernard Malamud on the themes of suffering and compassion and Flannery O'Connor as a "sharp analyst of our secular society." Even James Baldwin's *Another Country* was not so much social protest, Hicks said, as "a plea for love, the kind of love that can break through all barriers." He defined the themes of these writers as "identity, responsibility, suffering, salvation, love," but he also noted that William Styron, Vance Bourjaily, John Updike, and Shirley Ann Grau were writing books with these themes, which were the ones of great literature. Hicks also observed that "What distinguishes the postwar writers is that they have abstracted the situations they write about from the social problems of this era. They do not write about big business or national politics or any of the great centers of power; they leave such problems to the journalists—Eugene Burdick, Allen Drury, and the like. They go below the surface to try to discover the true nature of man." To Hicks, every good novel was "a protest against the dehumanization of life. It proclaims the significance of the individual against the machine and against the mechanization of society." This kind of novel was needed now, he said, and might be needed even more in the future.[4]

He again defended the function of the novel in 1967. The novel was not moribund, he said, "because it can explore problems of man's nature and man's fate that the physical and social sciences are compelled to ignore and that philosophy approaches only in a cold and formal fashion. What is man? To what values can he hold? What meaning has his life?" The traditional religions did not satisfy many people on these questions: "The novelist Dostoevsky professed orthodoxy, but his novels raised problems that orthodoxy couldn't touch. The most interesting of contemporary American novelists—Malamud, Ellison, Barth, and others—insist on scrutinizing fundamental issues."[5]

After retiring from the *Saturday Review* in 1969, Hicks continued to write occasional pieces and also to defend the novel. In "The Changing Novel," an address delivered to the Otto Rank Association in 1969 and published in its journal in 1970, Hicks speculated that the realistic novel might be declining; but he did not think that the genre itself was dying. After tracing the history of the novel from its beginning, Hicks suggested that the purely realistic novel had not been the dominant kind for a long time, although it still had its validity. Since even Hemingway was not a "naturalistic" writer nor even a realist in an exact sense, and since Faulkner was even less a naturalist, the novel was not declining, even though the truly realistic novel might be. Among remaining realists, he mentioned Cozzens and Auchincloss, who wrote about a settled class to whom manners were important. "I do not want to disparage Cozzens and Auchincloss, who do what they do very well; but they interest me less than Saul Bellow, Bernard Malamud, Wright Morris, John Updike, Flannery O'Connor, and various others, none of whom is a consistent realist."

The nonrealistic novel, Hicks continued, had a long history

that dated back to Laurence Sterne and that included James Joyce, as well as more recent writers such as Vladimir Nabokov, Anthony Burgess, Thomas Pynchon, John Barth, and Susan Sontag. "It seems clear that some of the most talented writers of our time have felt that realism did not give them a chance to express their peculiar awareness of the human condition." Several of them had made use of ancient myths, and others had mixed fantasy with realism. In this respect, Hicks mentioned Malamud's *The Natural*, Updike's *The Centaur*, Barth's *Giles Goat-Boy*, Ralph Ellison's *Invisible Man*, and Bellow's *Henderson the Rain King*.

Furthermore, the novel was important to Hicks because of the modern worship of technology, which resulted in a dehumanized interest in technique and in the decline of imagination. "A society that does not cherish the arts and lets them die is a sick society." Because our ability to put ourselves in another person's situation helped humanize us, Hicks stated that he was "concerned with the novel because it is one of the major expressions of imagination in our time. If the novel were dying, I should have even less hope for the future of our society than I have now."[6]

As late as 1975, when America began to celebrate its bicentennial, Hicks was defending and explaining the novel. The American Revolution and the English novel, he said in an article for the *American Way* (a magazine published by American Airlines to which he began contributing a monthly book column in July, 1973), had begun with the same generation of men. The novel had had, he said, "an increasingly important place in the culture of the Western World in the past two centuries, and American novels have come to stand with the best." But we seemed to have fewer good readers who were willing to meet the writers' heavier demands. The rewards of reading such demanding novels were correspondingly great, although most people never gave themselves a chance to find out. "Here is one of the many problems our first two centuries hand on to the future."[7] Hicks, who was still writing a good word for the novel, had become in these late years perhaps the most readable and prestigious of popular advocates of serious fiction.

II   *Refinements of Hicks's Theory*

Still making no effort to be a theoretician, Hicks from time to time made statements in his reviews which indicate that he had evolved a loose set of ideas on analyzing and evaluating literature. Moreover, he also made some improvements in his reviewing practice. In his first "Literary Horizons" column in 1958, he attempted again to define what critics and reviewers should do. The critic, he said, examined literature in the largest context with posterity in mind; but the reviewer lived and wrote in the present. The same person could be a critic and a reviewer, but the functions were different: "A review is a public transaction in which the author is really not involved, no matter how much pleasure or pain it may give him." The reviewer had to take the book for what it was, no matter how it was written. As for standards of expertise, Hicks noted that there were many types of excellence in writing and the more of them a reviewer could see, the better he could do his job. Since there were so many contradictory ideas about what was great in fiction, and since these ideas sometimes canceled each other, the reviewer had to "examine skeptically his own favorite formulas." Writers chose the standards their works were to be judged by, Hicks said, but the reviewer, who might have only minimal standards, still had to condemn "shoddiness, pretentiousness, dishonesty, and all the grosser kinds of failure. But any book that passes the elementary tests deserves to be examined and judged on its own terms."[8] Thus Hicks defined his tolerant, receptive approach to a book.

The question of response to a literary work—as opposed to the already discussed new criticism or academic analysis of it—appeared several times; and Hicks was, as we have observed, on the side of those who responded and who wanted to know as much as possible about the book, author, and background. Hicks said in 1962 that Graham Greene's book about his travels to Africa to research *A Burnt-Out Case* shed some light on the novel that was interesting and important. Strict textual explications rather than looking at all relevant information was bad; for, wrote Hicks, "There seems to me something sterile about criticism that is exclusively textual."[9]

He made his best statement on such a critical approach in "Art Lost in Analysis" (1967). When he was a student, Hicks said, instructors talked about the life of the writer, the social background, and other persons who influenced that writer. "The trouble was, of course, that the individual work of literature was often lost from sight" since it was easier to talk about the author, his circle, and his social background and since most students liked this approach because they could take many notes. The rebellion against this method had started in the 1920s, but then came the 1930s with the Marxist critical attack. When, by the end of World War II, Marxism's influence had passed, the new criticism, with its emphasis on the individual poem, play, or novel, became popular. "There is no doubt in my mind that on the whole the New Criticism has had a salutary effect on the teaching of literature. By always asking what a writer is trying to say, it helps the student to learn to read intelligently, and it opens his mind to literary virtues of which he may have been oblivious. It teaches him to concentrate on words, images, and symbols, the stuff out of which literature is made."

However, such "minute textual analysis" had its disadvantages for both teachers and for students, for ". . . in the hands of many teachers the New Criticism has become the New Pedantry. Just as in the old days it was easier to teach biography and history than to teach poetry or fiction, so now it is easier to teach images and symbols." This emphasis led to oversimplifying the meaning of a literary work, to avoiding "the contemplation of literature itself." Teachers could not teach the humanities like science, Hicks said, for the reader must react to values and use his imagination. Reading literature should be an experience—a disturbing but a satisfying one.[10]

III   His Critical Practice

From this set of general attitudes, Hicks practiced his "reviewing," but his discussions qualified in many ways under his definition of "criticism." Although much of Hicks's practice remained constant, some pertinent analysis of his later criticism can still be made to add to what we observed in chapter 7. He talked about the plot of a novel, of course, and tried to identify the theme. As he discussed the plausibility of the story and the relevance of the details, the writer who threw in extraneous details or sentimentalized was apt to be adversely criticized by Hicks. Furthermore, in keeping with his belief in the importance of background, he always identified the author as well as he could: what he had done in his previous novels, what Hicks thought of them, how they compared with the new book, and sometimes what his personal background was.

Hicks also took pains to define the tone of a novel, the author's attitude, and his view of life as expressed through his characters.

Of Kingsley Amis in his *My Enemy's Enemy*, for example, Hicks said that Amis, who was basically comic, showed more wit and used fewer of the kinds of gags found in Peter DeVries's novels. Amis, who gave a comic treatment of fundamentally serious themes, did so in a lighthearted way: "Much modern life he finds distasteful, and he says so in a cheerful but nevertheless emphatic fashion. Much he finds ridiculous, and he knows how to laugh and how to make others laugh." Amis avoided both complacency and despair in a world that seemed to offer only those alternatives, "and that in itself is a good deal to say," Hicks concluded.[11]

As for style and technique, Hicks mentioned whatever he thought was important—use of narrative point of view, figures of speech, even prose rhythm. Of Brian Moore's novel *I Am Mary Dunne*, for instance, he said that Moore chose rightly in having Mary tell her own story. It was the "style" that made the difference, for Mary's point of view dictated it. Elizabeth Spencer's *Knights and Dragons* had a distinguished style. After quoting a passage from the ending of the novel, he said, "Her style often suggests James's, but she has her own rhythms, her own way of using figures of speech, her own feeling for words."[12]

This quoting of passages from a novel or story did a great deal to improve his articles; for, as we noted in chapter 7, he seldom was able to do so in the 1950s. By 1963, he was taking more opportunities to quote from the books he was reviewing. This simple practical principle of being specific works well in book reviewing and in critical works. Too much of what passes as literary criticism is abstract and philosophical; and the author assumes that his reader really knows exactly what the critic is referring to. Reviewing can also be vague; but a quoted passage can enlighten the reader as nothing else does—and it did just that in Hicks's reviews.

IV   *The Duties of Writers*

When Hicks attempted to clarify his views about the duties of writers, he asserted in 1958 that writing was a discipline; and, when he stated that Edward Loomis had written a good novel in *End of a War*, it was, he said, "the opposite pole from those novels that present experience for experience's sake." (He probably was thinking of James Jones, whom he had attacked a few months earlier.) "The materials have been acted upon and transformed . . . and the result is something new." Loomis was not as good as Hemingway, but he had examined experience for himself and had done it well. "It is only apparently a paradox that in literature what is spontaneous is rarely original. When the undisciplined mind lets itself go, what comes out on paper is a hodgepodge of secondhand experiences."[13]

On this basis, Hicks was willing to forgive James Jones for his past sins when he published a short novel, *The Pistol*, which had the kind of discipline and the selectivity that was absent from *Some Came Running*. But two other novelists were the subject of his scorn in 1960 when they failed to exercise discipline and to achieve good form. In his review of James Barlow's *The Patriots*, Hicks wrote that, "To find the best way to tell a story, you have to be clear about the story you want to tell, and Barlow wasn't." Hicks also said that Anthony West in *The Trend Is Up* had written "an old-fashioned, sprawling kind of biographical novel, full of episodes that are irrelevant to the central theme." Because the writers of the 1950s knew about form and had practiced good form for the most part, their work made these two novels an embarrassment.[14]

V   *The Contents of Fiction*

Besides talking of what critics and authors ought to do, Hicks had some thoughts on three things that fiction contains: ideas, feeling, and information. He was always interested in all three, but he came to believe that depth of feeling was perhaps the most important element. John O'Hara in *From the Terrace* relied too much on facts and did not carry the reader into the feelings of characters; Hicks noted, as an example, that O'Hara expected his readers to accept his assertion of love at first sight.[15]

Hicks agreed with Harry Levin in a book on Hawthorne, Poe, and Melville that some of our best writers display a symbolic quality and a "dark wisdom." Although Levin said that these authors are the great creators, Hicks's response was, "Well, yes and no, but in any case it is a valid way." It was, however, a good thing that writers did say the darker things besides what the molders of public opinion wanted us to believe. "There is a darkness in all great writers, even in those who, like Tolstoy, eventually arrive at some grand affirmation."[16]

Revealing his regard for feeling over facts, Hicks said that a novel about the Caribbean by Albert Guerard did not create in him a feeling for or about the characters. True, it had authoritative information and good technique. "Guerard had the material and he had the technical skill, and he went to work. I don't much care what happens to any of these people, and he doesn't seem to either. The moral problem that is raised . . . is something to talk about, not something to feel deeply."[17] In another case, Hicks expressed his preference for Malamud over John Cheever on the basis of depth of feeling: "This is not a complaint: he [Cheever] has, as I have been trying to say, other virtues. But when one reads Bernard Malamud's *Rembrandt's Hat* . . . one sees what Cheever can't do—or perhaps doesn't want to."[18]

That books are more than just social and political ideas or moral issues was a lesson that Hicks's radical criticism of the 1930s had taught him. This fact does not mean, however, that Hicks did not care for ideas and moral issues in fiction; for he did. John Fowles's novel *The Collector* was not only a bizarre melodrama, he said, but also a novel that looked critically at contemporary England. Hicks, ever on the alert for expressions of serious ideas and insights, quoted the captured girl in the story to show her attitude toward her captor and toward the people who are against quality, excellence, and uniqueness: "She is a dedicated student of art, a pacifist out of love of life, a foe of convention, a foe of mediocrity."[19]

When reviewing a novelist of morals like Graham Greene, Hicks clearly relished his discussion and handled the ideas with ease. In *The Comedians*, Greene dealt with a committed Catholic and a group of uncommitted characters. Although Greene showed understanding for all of them, Hicks observed that Greene was on the side of the committed ones. But Hicks then elaborated: "What seems to me new in the novel is the breadth of sympathy that Greene shows. . . . He seems to recognize, as he has not in most of his books, that, though evil is evil, there are many kinds of good."[20] The ideas and the information are fine, Hicks implied, but feeling is still the touchstone. The review also illustrates Hicks's dealing with a writer's attitudes, as did his comments about Cheever and Fowles.

VI   *New Types of Novels*

As new types of novels emerged in the 1960s, Hicks supported them, although he still liked the more traditional ones as well; and he evinced some impatience with the "far-out" types. Concerning the merits of the novel of character, Hicks asserted in 1959 that Angus Wilson's *The Middle Age of Mrs. Wilson* showed the strength of the character novel. The French critic Alain Robbe-Grillet had said that this type of fiction belonged to the past because of the depersonalization of modern life and the lack of importance of individuals in shaping history. Hicks admitted that depersonalization was present in our age and noted that such novelists as Franz Kafka, Samuel Beckett, John Paul Sartre, and Albert Camus had effectively explored the phenomenon of the modern age's threat to individual personality. Yet, Hicks said, ". . . in spite of . . . Robbe-Grillet, most of us are more interested in people than in anything else, and it is because we are interested in people that we are interested in novels." Wilson's novel was "further evidence of the continuing vitality of the traditional novel."[21]

But in 1964 he seemed less certain about the value of the older type and more receptive to the newer. C. P. Snow was wrong in denouncing new types of novels, he said; but Hicks still liked Snow a lot in practice—although he found Snow's novels less exciting than the new types or even Anthony Powell's realistic novels, which were influenced by the kinds Snow did not like. Snow's style was clear but dull: "His style is magnificently lucid, but it offers few images and little excitement. His technique owes nothing to Joyce or Virginia Woolf or Lawrence or any of the other writers who brought the modern novel into existence. His characters are sharply defined and seldom give the reader much sense of the mystery of personality." Literary life would be barren, Hicks said, without the newer types. At the same time, Snow's interest in how conscience operates in high places was "a proper field for the operation of the imagination."[22]

The new, difficult novels gave Hicks some trouble, although he tried to be as open and receptive as he could. Susan Sontag in 1963 prompted him to ask, "But why did Miss Sontag, with her unmistakable talents, her great care, her thoughtfulness, write *The Benefactor*? To show something, one can say, about the mystery of personality. But what is she trying to show? Why does she elude the reader at every corner? Why has she made herself as great a mystery as the man she is writing about? Much modern fiction is difficult, some of it in an arbitrary and even perverse way. Why do we bother to read it? Actually, I am afraid, not many people will read *The Benefactor*, but the book is a challenge. One respects Miss Sontag's seriousness and her abilities as a writer so much that one wants to give her the benefit of every doubt."[23]

When Donald Barthelme published his first book of short stories, *Come Back, Dr. Caligari* (1964), Hicks said that he was "a member of the advance guard, and he is very far out indeed." These stories which belonged to "the literature of absurdity," were not always successful. "But a good deal of the time Barthelme manages to evoke the kind of thoughtful laughter he is looking for, the kind of astonishment that is a stimulant." His new effects made him important as an experimentalist, for he might be "showing literature a new path to follow."[24]

In dealing with three "far-out" novels, Hicks said in 1969 that one was a failure, one a partial success, and a third (which did not stray completely from tradition) was good. Rudolph Wurlitzer's novel *Nog* he dismissed as dull. He was partly entertained, however, by John Leonard's *Crybaby of the Western World* with its puns and gags, such as this line from a poem: "A slice of Hamlet on wry toast." "Only a writer of unusual fortitude could keep up this sort of thing for 254 pages, but Leonard is tireless even though the reader may not be. The effect is sometimes genuinely Joycean, but more often Leonard sounds like a hungover gag writer for a TV show." Of Marilyn Hoff's good novel, he said, "*Rose* is by any standard a novel of some distinction. We may not understand why Martin and Jane choose to live as they do, but they are real and likable and we want to know what happens to them. I have nothing against experiments such as Leonard's and Wurlitzer's, but I am glad that Miss Hoff, who is something of an experimenter in her own way, has not found it necessary to sacrifice all the standards of the traditional novel. If her journeying has taken her far out, she has not lost her ability to communicate with the people back home."[25]

VII   *New Themes*

When Hicks talked about the new themes that had developed in fiction in the 1950s and 1960s, he observed that chief among these was the "mystery of personality" that has already been mentioned in two instances. In his 1960 essay, "As Fiction Faces the Sixties," he also suggested that writers should be allowed to seek their own themes and that it was fortunate that writers did not follow the advice of critics but instead did what they had to do. "What they have mostly done is to explore the human spirit under pressure. It is, I think, the theme that the era has given them, and the best have done a great deal with it."[26]

In "The Personality Paradox" (1960), in which Hicks discussed new approaches to personality, he observed that many writers suggested that reality and personality were perceived only in fragments or from certain points of view, and that such glimpses or views presented *a* truth but not *the* truth: "Many novelists today do not see character quite as their predecessors did. Physics, sociology, and especially psychology have made it difficult to define sharply the boundaries of the individual. Moreover, rapidity of technological change, the increase in social mobility, and the constant exposure to other cultures have eroded those boundaries. Although the great writers have always recognized and meditated upon the mystery of personality, in earlier times . . . it was easier to feel that personality was stable." Character today seemed to be seen by writers as in flux, and in this connection he mentioned Saul Bellow and Wright Morris.[27]

Also in relation to themes, Hicks contributed an essay, "Generations of the Fifties: Malamud, Gold, and Updike," to a book entitled *The Creative Present* (1963). In it he suggested that Malamud, Updike, and Herbert Gold had as their primary preoccupation the theme of redemption, which they saw as coming from within the person, not from society.[28] In another example, Hicks mentioned in 1966 that Iris Murdoch seemed to be suggesting in her novels that the world is not what it seems to be.[29] New themes and new kinds of novels were emerging, and Hicks was contributing his insights in accounting for them.

VIII   *Faulkner, Hemingway, Wilder, Fitzgerald*

Hicks's treatment of four of America's older authors—Faulkner, Hemingway, Wilder, and Fitzgerald—will help to indicate further the nature of his criticism during this period. William Faulkner was the subject of a few pieces by Hicks during the 1960s and 1970s, his review of *The Reivers* (1962) being an example of his treatment. It was a good novel, Hicks said—better than *The Mansion* or *The Town*; the narrator had better control than in the Gavin Stevens sections of the other novels, and it was like *Intruder in the Dust* in manner and tone because it had a sense of excitement. "There is in the book none of the demonic power and little of the dazzling originality of the half dozen great books [by Faulkner] that appeared from 1929 to 1943, but there is excitement, and there is humor, and there is a strong moral sense."[30]

Reviewing a collection of essays on Faulkner in 1967, Hicks suggested that Faulkner was relevant to our times, for he had attacked modernity in his novels. He had attacked, for example, the evil things in modern industrial society that were exemplified by the characters Jason Compson, Flem Snopes, and Roth Edmonds. ". . . Faulkner pointed to the qualities in contemporary life that seemed to him destructive. On the other hand, he found in some of the men of the Old World virtues that civilization may not be able to do without. Faulkner was uncomfortable when he had to deal directly with problems of the modern world, but he had already made indirect comments of high cogency. It takes a long time to exhaust the relevance of a great writer, and as time goes on we are likely to find more that is significant for us in Faulkner, not less."[31]

When Ernest Hemingway died in 1961, Hicks wrote a tribute to him which contained some astute comments about Hemingway's books and his possible motives for suicide. Hemingway personified the revolt of the 1920s with his simple code built on courage and individualism—themes and characteristics which had made him a legend among the "organization men" of recent decades. Hicks cited the quote from Shakespeare's Henry IV, part 2, as important in Hemingway's confrontation with death: "By my troth, I care not; a man can but die once; we owe God a death and let it go which way it will he that dies this year is quit for the next." With the aid of Shakespeare, Hicks said, Hemingway had conquered the fear of dying, but it was as if "from that time on, he had to test himself again and again to make sure the victory was still his. And perhaps in the end, having grown weary of forcing himself to the test, he embraced the thing itself." Hemingway had portrayed this age of violence and had "stood for individualism in an age of conformity. But his greatness had little to do with this particular age. It depended on his singular ability to feel and express the simplest of all facts, the fact of death."[32]

Thornton Wilder, whom radicals such as Hicks had attacked during the 1930s, received a Hicks tribute in a 1973 review of *Theophilus North*. To Hicks, each of Wilder's books had always been a new departure, and this "novel made up of short stories" was another. The character North was the unifying element in each story, and Wilder had hit upon the device of giving him access to many kinds and classes of people by making him a teacher of tennis and a reader of many languages in Newport, Rhode Island. North, who went about helping people, became a kind of quiet saint. "Wilder's tone remains consistently lively, is often comic, and the book is extraordinarily entertaining," Hicks said. "There are those . . . who will call it corny, and sometimes it comes wrecklessly close to sentimentality. . . . But in spite of an excess of sweetness now and then . . . the stories hold the reader in a firm grip."

Wilder was, Hicks observed, instinctively an optimistic person. "At the same time there is in his makeup a tough streak of pessimism." His books have all shown this pessimism because his optimism "operates only in the short run, for his view of man's fate is by no means cheerful. But he does see that there are happy passages along life's way, and he seems to believe that we should make the most of them, not merely in the sense of seizing the day but also as experiences to be taken into account in our judgment of the human condition. . . . What Theophilus North learns in Newport is that most people could be happier than they are, and experimentation teaches him that sometimes he can improve their lot."[33] This passage represents Hicks at his best—lucid, astute, informative.

With the release in 1974 of the new movie based on F. Scott Fitzgerald's *The Great Gatsby*, Hicks wrote an article in which he tried to put the novel in perspective—and he did an admirable job. He traced Fitzgerald's career, pointed out that the novel was his least autobiographical, and asserted that it was more a love story than a story of the Jazz Age. He said the novel was beautifully composed and that Nick Carraway as narrator served well, and then he turned to its themes: "The first theme, the great romance, is symmetrically developed, with the movement upward exactly balanced by the movement downward." The second theme is wealth—old and new—with Tom Buchanan representing established money and Gatsby the vulgar new rich. Gatsby became tired of being a spendthrift, and Daisy became "not merely the object of love but also the meaning of his life." Gatsby proved true to his ideal, although it led to tragedy; and he was better than Tom, Daisy, the others. But the novel, Hicks said, went further in theme than great love and the integrity of Gatsby. For "Gatsby's story symbolizes the exploitation of the American continent. But more than that. . . . In the end, then, what the book is really about is the vanity of human wishes."

Fitzgerald's portrait of Gatsby was a masterpiece, he said, and Fitzgerald knew it and later regretted that he had not followed in its path with greater dedication. "He not only found the form that would make us see Gatsby and feel his impact; symbol and image deepened his narrative, so that a somewhat sordid story speaks to us of the human condition. It is no wonder that some years passed before critics grasped the full extent of his achievement." This novel was Fitzgerald's best work. "It is startling—and saddening, too—to think that in 1925, before he was thirty, Fitzgerald had reached the climax of his career. . . . Only in the very best of the short stories, and perhaps in the promise of the novel he was working on at the time of his death, *The Last Tycoon*, was he to come anywhere near the mark *Gatsby* had set."[34]

IX   *Morris, Malamud, Bellow*

Wright Morris, Bernard Malamud, and Saul Bellow were the three writers that Hicks liked most of those who had developed after World War II. A review of his comments on these authors—one that adds to the remarks about them that have already been cited—best reflects his literary tastes in these later years and also indicates his broadened approach, his continued interest in novels about moral ideas, and his enunciation of literary themes. Wright Morris, whom Hicks had been interested in since Morris's first novel in 1942, received a lot of attention from Hicks. *Literary Horizons, A Quarter Century of American Fiction* (1970) has forty pages on Morris that were taken from Hicks's reviews over the years. Morris seemed to him to be one of our important writers but one who had been neglected by the reading public. Hicks wrote one of his best late pieces of sustained criticism about Morris in the twenty-four page introduction to *Wright Morris: A Reader* (1970). Since then, he has favorably reviewed Morris's later novels.

Perhaps the best way to represent briefly Hicks's view of Morris is to cite some of his different comments from the introduction to the *Reader*. "We have here," Hicks said, "the results of more than

twenty-five years of disciplined productivity, to be read and enjoyed and meditated upon." The plains helped shape Morris, he
said; they mean to him what the sea meant to Melville and Conrad—a symbol of the universe. Some of Morris's recurrent themes
as seen by Hicks were "the relativity of all knowledge, nostalgia
and the general problem of the past, the possibilities of human
transformation, and the role of heroism." "Morris finds people
frequently pathetic, often terribly exasperating, and endlessly
fascinating. There are no villains and no heroes of the romantic
sort, but Morris does have heroes of his own variety. That is,
there are characters who are set apart from the mass of men by
virtue of special qualities." Most of his heroes, audacious and
bold, refuse to accept "the limitations by which most men are
held prisoner"; but, while some characters are "audaciously active, others are disturbingly passive." Objects attract Morris, he
said, but for a reason: "Morris never calls attention to an artifact
simply because it happens to be occupying space; it must have
done something to his imagination. . . . Things are important
when they speak for men."

Morris is skillful, Hicks continued, in solving problems of form;
he is good at handling time and in manipulating narrative point
of view. "The rhythms of his prose . . . are basically the rhythms
of ordinary talk." "This flexible, conversational, amusing, un-
pretentious style, which is in fact extremely artful, can serve
many purposes." "Cliches are an essential part of Morris's
style . . . he uses them for his own purposes." "Morris's figures of
speech . . . are usually derived from familiar artifacts or commonplace experiences, from the stuff of ordinary life." Though
his style bothers some people, "many of us" feel that "he has
forged an almost perfect instrument for the expression of his
understanding of life and his feeling about it."[35]

As these comments indicate, Hicks saw in Morris a writer who
felt and thought deeply about existence in the universe, about
isolation, and about human relationships. He suggested that Morris portrayed people as mysterious and complex, as mixtures of
good and bad. Hicks also emphasized Morris's comic inven-
tiveness, and he so appreciated the comedy of the novels that he
expressed his enjoyment of it more than he usually did in discussing novels. Perhaps Hicks took delight in these qualities because
he saw that Morris, while comic, ultimately returned to a serious
tone in his novels. Hicks was interested, in other words, in the

ideas and in the feelings he perceived that Morris was expressing; but he was also interested in and spent a great deal of space discussing Morris's techniques and form. His introduction to the Morris reader is one of Hicks's most thorough pieces of criticism, for it demonstrates the versatility and range that he could command in his mature period.

Although Hicks usually dealt more briefly with Bernard Malamud's work than with Morris's, Hicks gave him high marks. In 1958 Hicks indicated his knowledge of Malamud's novels in a review of *The Magic Barrel*: "It is in the world of Jewish storekeepers and their like that most of the stories in *The Magic Barrel* are laid. In *The Assistant*, which seems to me one of the important novels of the postwar period, Jewish experience is used as a way of approaching the deepest, broadest problems of love and fear, of communion and isolation in human life. So, too, in *The Magic Barrel*: the more faithfully Malamud renders Jewish life, the wider his meanings are. . . . The question Malamud asks more often than any other is: what are the limits of human responsibility?"[36]

In 1961, in a review of Malamud's *A New Life*, Hicks indicated that "The novel has a less immediate impact than *The Assistant*. There, in the relationship between Frank and the Bober family the situation is sharply defined, and the story rises to a dramatic and moving climax. But *A New Life* is larger in scope, and the problem to which it is addressed is a more profound one. Levin, as I have said, is a hero and very much a hero of our times. He has escaped from despair, only to find himself surrounded by triviality, but he has the courage to cling to what he believes."[37]

When Hicks wrote a long review in 1966 on Malamud's *The Fixer*, he called it "one of the finest novels of the postwar period"; but he hesitated to use the word "great" because of disagreement over the meaning of the word. As Hicks made clear, one academic critic had talked of John Barth's *Giles Goat-Boy* in that way and had argued that C. P. Snow and Saul Bellow did not fit with Joyce, Proust, Mann, and Faulkner, as did Barth. "What I am saying, of course, is what I have said before—that there are more kinds than one of literary merit and even greatness. I think *Giles Goat-Boy*, and *The Fixer*, are both unusually good and unusually important novels, though they have little in common except their excellence. Malamud has told a straightforward story in language of the greatest austerity." He concluded, "All of the scenes in *The*

Fixer . . . have been worked upon by a not merely compassionate but an anguished imagination. The style, which seems so simple, is a triumph of discipline; scarcely a word could be spared. *The Fixer* is a novel that offers a great experience, first of all a literary experience, but not merely that."[38]

In his foreword to the Malamud section in the book *Literary Horizons* (1970), Hicks more or less summarized his views of the author: "I cannot say that each book he has written has been an improvement over the last, but each book does represent growth in one way or another—style, form, depth of feeling, range of emotion. . . . It is suitable that his most recent novel, *Pictures of Fidelman*, is a subtle study of the character of the artist. One of his funniest books, it is also one of his most profound."[39]

For Saul Bellow, Hicks made larger claims about the greatness of some of the novels than they may deserve, especially *The Adventures of Augie March* and *Henderson the Rain King*. But Hicks has the virtue of informing, clarifying, and expanding our view of a novel without intimidating us into agreeing with him if we do not want to. In his foreword to the *Literary Horizons* section about Bellow, he said, "But it was *Augie March* that caught me, as it caught a large section of the reading public. Here was a man who had created a style for himself and unleashed an energy such as I had felt in only a few contemporary writers—the early Faulkner, for example."[40] In his review of the novel in 1953, he had said of Augie, "His central quality . . . is his determination to be himself, and the only difficulty is that . . . he doesn't know what he is. Whether he has found out by the end of the book is a question, but along the way at least he has learned a lot about what he isn't." He then observed that Augie was perceptive and convinced us that we live in exciting times.[41]

Of *Henderson the Rain King* he said in 1959 that Bellow had written, as he had in other stories, "an account of a man's struggle to find and to transcend himself." To Hicks, this book was "as exciting a novel as has appeared in a long time." "No one," he said, "has ever conveyed so well as Saul Bellow the anguish of a man who is capable of honestly contemplating his nature but incapable of changing it." It might not be a better book than *Augie March*, but it was "a book that should be read again and again, and each reading, I believe, will yield further evidence of Bellow's wisdom and power."[42] This lavish praise makes one wonder if Hicks might have again lapsed into a moral earnestness like that of his young days. He has always been in danger, in fact, of falling into his fervent old habits, although he has guarded against them and tried to judge novels coolly.

Hicks's assessment of *Herzog* in 1964 seems more valid. The letters that Moses Herzog writes, he said, were a device the author used for exploring Herzog's psyche. This method of presentation worked well, he said, but could have been dull. As Bellow handled the letters, they were "lively, sometimes profound, and always revelatory." The central character in *Seize the Day* had found hope for changing himself from a kind of mystical experience; Henderson had been redeemed by the African king's fantastic rites: "Herzog, on the other hand, seeks salvation by the way of the intellect. . . . He is driven . . . but he is not driven blindly"—as the other characters are. Hicks concluded that "*Herzog* re-enforces my conviction that Bellow is the leading figure in American fiction today."[43]

In his afterword to *Literary Horizons*, Hicks paid tribute to *Mr. Sammler's Planet*, a work which he had not reviewed: it was "the finest novel Bellow has written and validates his claim to preeminence among contemporary writers of fiction. Like *Herzog*, it is a novel of ideas, but here the thinker is mature, resolute, and uncomplaining. Although he has seen too much of the world to underestimate the powers of evil, Sammler is grateful for good wherever he may find it."[44] Although Hicks showed in these comments that he was still moved by novels that carried a serious moral force and that dealt with ideas, his views about the novel seem particularly apt.

When Bellow's novel *Humboldt's Gift* appeared, Hicks said in 1975 in a long review that he placed Bellow near the top of America's living novelists but that the new novel "does less for Bellow's reputation than I had hoped. On the other hand, the novel does not damage his reputation as much as some of my specific comments might seem to suggest." Hicks praised Bellow for his wide knowledge, for his ability to use it with ease in his novels, and also for his mastery of style, "without ever yielding, as John Updike sometimes does, to the temptation to show off." Hicks took some pains to quote several passages from the novel, to explain various aspects of the plot, and then to call into question the plausibility of certain behavior, especially that of Charlie Citrine, the main character: "Many questions are left unanswered: Why, for instance, is Citrine both so docile and so fearless in performing the acts of contrition Cantible imposes on him? . . . I don't believe Bellow needs to put that burden on his readers; he can tell a straight story when he wants to. And he can suggest a state of mind as no one else can."[45] The review is informative, it raises some helpful questions, and it also challenges the writer who creates needless problems for his readers.

X   Taking on Mailer and Company

With Norman Mailer, Hicks was often involved in controversy. To Mailer, Hicks was one of those critics who was always wrong. Although Hicks may have felt distressed and secretly angered, he always tried to present Mailer in a balanced, fair way. He remarked in 1960 that Mailer and Leslie Fiedler were too self-conscious in their rebellion and in their saying "No." They served a useful purpose, he said, but they were too afraid to be agreed with, and they constantly felt compelled to shock their audiences.[46]

The critical squabble in 1965 over Mailer's novel *An American Dream* was the most noteworthy Mailer controversy in which Hicks became involved. Reviewing Mailer's career, he said that *The Naked and the Dead* was clumsy in spots, that it was imitative of Dos Passos and Hemingway, but that it was "the best American novel about World War II and . . . the most remarkable exhibition in recent times of the naturalistic technique." Since its appearance in 1948, Mailer had not done very well: *Barbary Shore* had been "an honorable failure"; *The Deer Park* had been greatly admired but, on the whole, was not a success. Mailer was still taken seriously, Hicks said, in spite of his failures; for example, Diana Trilling in *The Living Present* had suggested that Mailer had a religious motive, that he was seeking a moral vision that transcended his hipsterism, and that he was on a religious crusade. Hicks said he wondered what she made of *An American Dream*; for, to Hicks, "If the book is not a joke, a bad joke, it is something worse." Having summarized the story, he stated the novel's absurdity was not just limited to the plot. The main character, Stephen Rojack, was a superman, an intellectual, and a good fighter—and had no reality: "We don't believe in him as a Congressman or as a professor or even as a lover; he exists as a projection of Norman Mailer's fantasies about himself. He is Mailer, as Mailer would like to be. The other characters are but dummies for Mailer-Rojack to manipulate." The writing was "the sloppiest Mailer has ever done," and Hicks quoted a passage to illustrate. Hicks, who scoffed at Mrs. Trilling's comments about Mailer, wondered how long she would be able to see him holding, in her words, "his place in the forefront of modern writers."[47]

Hicks was offended by Mailer's novel for several reasons. Having been very much a rationalist during his career, Hicks found repugnant the kind of mindless violence and juvenile sexual fantasies that he found in the book—the probing of supposedly instinctive nonrational forces which Diana Trilling liked. One *Saturday Review* reader wrote a letter attacking Hicks for not liking the novel and its "new paths in language," and called him "a stodgy moralist" (July 3, 1965). Hicks was something of a moralist, but he was not stodgy. His praise of Philip Roth's *Portnoy's Complaint* undercuts that accusation, for Hicks said the use of profane language by Roth was entirely apt. "This story could not be told without the use of what were once known as obscenities," he said in his afterword to the Roth section in *Literary Horizons*.[48] Although Hicks has admitted to being "an old fogey," he was willing to tolerate artistically justified obscenity and sex in literature, but he chose to conduct himself personally with old-fashioned rectitude.

The controversy over Mailer's novel raged among the critics, and Hicks wrote another piece concerning it a few weeks later. He defended his choice of Bellow's *Herzog* as a good novel and Mailer's as "an uncommonly bad novel." The critic Richard Poirier had tried to make a case for Mailer's great style, but, to Hicks, Poirier quoted "long passages full of ineptitude" to prove it. The other critics, who had pertinent things to say about Mailer's intentions, had mistaken "intention for achievement." For example, such critics said that Mailer was trying to create a hero and a modern myth; but Rojack, to Hicks, was "no more a hero than his creator, who resembles him in many ways and would be glad, I am sure, to resemble him in more." Mailer had said that love was something for which one paid a big price, "But what evidence is there that Mailer, who knows quite a lot about sex, knows anything about love?" After explaining why he liked *Herzog*, Hicks said that Mailer's Rojack as a character had ideas that were either trivial or absurd but that Bellow's Herzog, on the other hand, was a thoughtful character who had been given life by a thoughtful author. "When one compares the intellectual richness of *Herzog* with the mindlessness of *An American Dream*, one has some measure of Bellow's superiority."[49]

In spite of this harshness, Hicks felt that Mailer was talented. When he reviewed the novel *Why Are We in Vietnam?* he panned the book but also said, "Why do we—why do I—go on bothering with Norman Mailer? Not merely because he once had talent, but because he still has it. There are passages in this book that nobody else could have written—as well as passages that, I hope, nobody else would have written."[50] He also liked Mailer's nonfiction books, *The Armies of the Night* and *Miami and the Siege of Chicago*. All in all, Hicks's comments about Mailer were pertinent—and also revealed the kind of critic Hicks was. He stubbornly held to certain rationalist, moralist traditions and tastes; and he found the violence and egocentricity in Mailer offensive. As to whether or not he reacted too negatively, that decision cannot yet be made, not only because Mailer's career has not ended, but also because his critical reputation still remains a matter of debate.

XI   *Other Novelists*

Hicks had useful things to say about many other novelists of this later period. He recognized John Barth as important, and he especially praised *The Sot-Weed Factor* and *Giles Goat-Boy*, which he called "one of the most important novels of our time."[51] He considered John Updike a promising writer; he kept thinking for a while that Updike could do better than he had; but, finding *A Month of Sundays* enjoyable and well written, he was more and more pleased as Updike continued to produce.[52] Hicks wrote balanced, informative reviews about Vladimir Nabokov's books, but he did not care for the way Nabokov played games with his readers.[53] He suggested that James Baldwin showed promising talent as a novelist in *Go Tell It on the Mountain* and in *Giovanni's Room*; that he had found in his nonfiction *In Another Country* the "appropriate rhetoric" for his "deep passion" on racial matters; but that he had written nothing else of importance.[54] He had mild praise for Philip Roth's *Letting Go* and *When She Was Good* and called *Portnoy's Complaint* "something very much like a masterpiece" primarily, as we have noted, because of Roth's creative use of obscene language.[55]

Hicks said that Herbert Gold "at his best always arouses my admiration," and he praised especially *The Man Who Was Not With It*, *Fathers*, and *The Great American Jackpot*.⁵⁶ Reynolds Price, he said, was good but had a limited range, and he named *A Long and Happy Life* and *A Generous Man* as successful and *Love and Work* as an unsuccessful departure.⁵⁷ As for Joseph Heller's *Catch 22*, he recognized it as part of the history of the 1960s but admitted that he had been bored with its many labored gags; but Heller's *Something Happened* did not have anything like the good parts of the first novel.⁵⁸ Kurt Vonnegut, Jr., he classified as a "desperate humorist" and an amusing satirist, and he considered his *Slaughterhouse-Five* to be "a masterpiece of indirection."⁵⁹ Thomas Pynchon's novel *V* was successful at showing "the chaotic complexity of life," but *The Crying of Lot 49* was "considerably easier to follow," was "just as funny" as the first novel, and was also a successful "nonrealistic novel."⁶⁰ Hicks praised John Gardner's work, finding *Grendel* to be "a remarkable tour de force," and *The Sunlight Dialogues* to be "complex and witty"; and *Nickel Mountain*, which was very good in its simplicity, had a memorable main character.⁶¹

During this last period of his career, Hicks was an open-minded critic, but one who still took his literature seriously—a critic who sought wisdom in his reading and who was offended by novelists who did not see fiction as serious or who used the novel as Mailer had in *An American Dream*. A critical reviewer, of course, is always gambling because he must make immediate judgments about books whose value will be judged in a larger perspective as time passes. But Hicks will probably sustain a high reputation because he always had important things to say; he refused to be tied too closely to any doctrine; and he approached fiction with many years of experience and practice behind him. In his last two decades, he offered perhaps his most valuable contribution to American literature. These years were a fitting crown to a noble career.

CHAPTER 9

Final Assessment

MANY years have passed since Granville Hicks decided that he was willing to dedicate his life to literary criticism rather than to liberal religion. As a result, he became a part of the literary and intellectual history of part of this century. During the late 1920s, by asserting the value of social morality in literature, he helped shape the critical dialogue of the time; but he was then far too unschooled to be an important figure. In the 1930s, he practiced a shallow Marxist criticism, but he was so centrally involved in the critical debates that he made a contribution to literary discussion in America. Having been disillusioned and chastened by the collapse of Communist credibility, he learned from his mistaken simplistic enthusiasm; and he not only gradually came to terms in the 1940s with literature on a nondoctrinaire basis but also explored with admirable astuteness the problems of the small town in America. From his early decades of experience, from his voluminous reading, and from his sobering adventures with politics, he became a wisely skeptical but humane person. As a result, during the 1950s, 1960s, and 1970s, Hicks was not only an important spokesman for the anti-Communist liberal position but also a flexible and useful critic—one who has not received the recognition he deserves because he is still associated with his excesses of the 1930s.

During the last twenty-five years of his career, Hicks found what he could do best: present to the reading public an open-minded, informed, and incisive view of recent fiction. The bulk of Hicks's work had to do with novels just published, and he reviewed them for his readers who wanted to decide whether or not to read them. He performed this function very, very well. In addition, his discussions of books were also valuable after we had read the books; for if we take a novel we already know and turn to a Hicks review of it, we will probably learn something. Thus,

150

Hicks's critical reviewing qualifies in most cases not just as literary journalism of a high order but also as permanent criticism. His was a happy combination of a suitable choice of subject, of a humble sense of high purpose, and of a persistent devotion to the task. American literature is the richer for the result.

Hicks has not given us any new theoretical tools, as did Wayne Booth, nor has he shown the intellectual depth of Edmund Wilson. He seldom went any deeper into a problem or a literary work than was immediately necessary; but he went deep enough to be illuminating. Above all, he was a sensible, balanced, and engaging critic who was unwilling in later years to follow the fads of criticism. He was open-minded about many kinds of books, whether they were in vogue with the critical establishment or not.

Morton D. Zabel said that criticism had achieved in the 1940s and 1950s a status that was aggressive and formidable, and much of it needed and received protest and reaction against it. Hicks is one of those who protested, especially against the abuses of the formalist critical approach in scholarly studies and in teaching— the "New Pedantry" he called it. Hicks would agree with Zabel that "The practical question remains one of the almost unprecedented lengths to which the critical function has been carried in our time; of the degree to which analytical and diagnostic techniques have outpaced mature insight and understanding; of the extent to which criticism has lost its contact with the vital experience—thought, imagination, emotion, vision—in which art of any valid kind originates; and of the risk the critic runs when his ingenuity or intellectual ambition exceeds his sympathy and *rapport* with the object to which he applies them."[1] Hicks addressed himself to precisely this problem and tried to avoid it in his critical reviewing.

Zabel, in trying to classify the work of American critics at midcentury, said there were five types of specialists at work. Then he added another category: "And against these specialists in method there must be counted the students who aim to restore a broader program of human and realistic values to the examination of literature in order to correct the specialization of aesthetic, technical, and archetypal approaches: thus the defenders of a revived historical and humanistic view of literature. . . ."[2] Hicks belongs in this or a similar category. He was more than a mere impressionist, "an adventurer among masterpieces." Though subjective in his approach, he did eclectically absorb some of the lessons taught us by the more specialized critics; but we have seen that he refused to be held to any system after he had rejected Marxism.

As a stylist Hicks is, at his best, lucid and amiable. He is readable, and he speaks with some force and wit when he is sure of himself, as he came more and more to be. When we read one of Hicks's articles, we feel we are in good company, in touch with a human being who is responding honestly and warmly to his subject. We are not likely, however, to be devastated by Hicks's wit, awestruck by his genius, or intimidated by an aggressively stated argument. We are not, in short, in the company of an H. L. Mencken, an Edmund Wilson, or a Norman Mailer. We are more likely to feel at ease with Hicks—and to be interested in being informed but not afraid to differ from his honestly stated and openly arrived at opinion. Hicks as a person and as a writer makes us feel comfortable.

At times Hicks's writing style was weakened by a tentative tone, an uneven rhythm, and a cloudy abstraction—and this last characteristic appears usually when he was not sure of himself. He was also too fond of "there is" and "it is" constructions: "It is safe to assume that there will be large numbers of serious and talented writers in the Sixties just as there have been in the Fifties." This syntax is often combined with such lapses as double negatives: "If, as I believe, there is something to look forward to on the farther side of mass culture, it is because the spirit of true art cannot be conquered. Even if a genius does come along, we cannot afford not to be grateful to the men and women of talent and dedication."

Seldom does his writing style break into a brutal frankness that is a characteristic of a George Orwell, nor does he express a robust or lusty sense of the comic in life. He probably put people at ease with his honest confessions of bafflement or mistake; but his humility also invited some scorn and condescension. Unfortunately, some human beings mistake honesty and humility for weakness. Furthermore, such hackneyed phrases as "casts its spell," "the human predicament," and "a deeply revealing book" occur often in his writing. But these expressions are very hard to avoid in something like literary journalism. The many examples from his works quoted here indicate that Hicks usually expressed himself quite well. His is not a thundering style but a clear and serviceable one.

As the bibliography of this book shows, and as we have observed in previous chapters, Hicks's books range from literary criticism and biography through fiction to nonfiction about society and about his own experiences. To summarize his achievements in them, we recognize that his first critical book, *The Great Tradition*, is an interesting but simplistic attempt at Marxist criticism. In his second attempt, *Figures of Transition*, he presents a very respectable piece of "Marxist" analysis. *John Reed: The Making of a Revolutionary* is a good biography of Reed, but his polemical *I Like America* is an embarrassingly naive attempt to win Americans over to communism by sweet reason. His utopian novel, *The First To Awaken*, is a creditable example of that genre, and his three novels about small town life—*Only One Storm*, *Behold Trouble*, and *There Was a Man in Our Town*—are interesting but only mildly successful. His nonfiction *Small Town* is an excellent book, the quintessence of Hicks's social wisdom. And his autobiographical books, *Where We Came Out* and *Part of the Truth*, are useful historical documents. Hicks's periodical essays and, as we have said, his reviews are valuable along with his books—perhaps in some ways more valuable. A reading of any of Hicks's essays listed in the bibliography or of the reviews collected in the book *Literary Horizons* will attest to their merit.

Human beings have responded warmly to Granville Hicks—whether reader, house guest, author, or student. He has proven to be a good friend, an honest and open-minded person, and a man who stuck to his principles and went about doing what he believed was important: looking steadily and devotedly at the unfolding of the novel in America; taking an interest in his friends, his town, his country; and contemplating the perilous journey of Western man in an era of momentous spiritual and physical change.

Notes and References

1. "Granville Hicks," *Current Biography*, 3 (May, 1942), 43–46.
2. *Part of the Truth* (New York, 1965), pp. 3–14.
3. Ibid., p. 8.
4. "The Natural History of an Intellectual," in *Small Town* (New York, 1946), pp. 21–22.
5. Ibid., p. 19.
6. Ibid., pp. 20–27.
7. Ibid., p. 27.
8. Ibid., pp. 28–30.
9. *Part of the Truth*, pp. 42–56.
10. *Small Town*, pp. 32–33.
11. *Part of the Truth*, p. 61.
12. *Where We Came Out* (New York, 1954), pp. 27–30; see also *Part of the Truth*, pp. 65–67, and *Small Town*, pp. 34–37.
13. "The Parsons and the War," *American Mercury*, February, 1927, pp. 129–42.
14. *Part of the Truth*, p. 59.
15. Ibid., pp. 75–82.
16. "Edmund Wilson," in *American Writers, A Collection of Literary Biographies* (New York, 1974), IV, 426–29.
17. "Malcolm Cowley," in *Contemporary Authors*, rev. ed. (Detroit, 1969), V–VIII, 257–59; conversation with Hicks on October 6, 1974.
18. Hicks gave me this personal information plus subsequent facts about his finances and ways of making a living when I interviewed him for this book on September 14 and 15, 1973.
19. *Part of the Truth*, pp. 102–5.
20. Ibid., pp. 130–33, on losing his job; on his social life, see especially pp. 106, 135; on his guests, see the index; on Yaddo, see p. 210.
21. Much of this information came directly from Hicks; but see also *Part of the Truth*, pp. 89–91 on Macmillan; p. 253 on the *New Leader*; pp. 277–78 on the New School and getting into New York; and pp. 284–85 on New York University and the *Saturday Review*.

Chapter Two

1. Review of *The Modern Temper*, by Joseph Wood Krutch, *Forum*, June, 1929, pp. x–xii.

2. "The Gutter—And Then What?" *Forum*, December, 1928, pp. 802, 809, 810.

3. Review of *Adam, the Baby and the Man from Mars*, by Irwin Edman, *Forum*, September, 1929, p. xvi.

4. Review of *The Whirligig of Taste*, by E. E. Kellett, *Nation*, March 27, 1929, p. 378.

5. Review of *Good-Bye to All That*, by Robert Graves, *New Freeman*, 1 (April 12, 1930), 117.

6. "Industry and the Imagination," *South Atlantic Quarterly*, 28 (April, 1929), 126–35.

7. "The Catholic Enigma," *Nation*, April 10, 1929, pp. 428–29; "Religion," *Nation*, October 23, 1929, pp. 469–70.

8. Review of *Humanism*, ed. Norman Foerster, *Forum*, March, 1930, pp. vi–viii.

9. Review of *Five Masters, A Study in the Mutations of the Novel*, by Joseph Wood Krutch, *New Republic*, November 26, 1930, pp. 50–51.

10. "The Past and Future of Poetry," *Nation*, February 6, 1929, pp. 165–66.

11. "The American Tragedy," *New Republic*, June 18, 1930, pp. 131–32.

12. "American Caravanserai," *New Republic*, April 1, 1931, pp. 185–86.

13. Review of *The Whirligig of Taste*, pp. 376–78.

14. Review of "The Passing of James Huneker," *Nation*, December 25, 1929, p. 780.

15. "Second Judgment," *Contempo*, 1 (January 1, 1932), 1–2.

16. "The Dilemma of a Critic," *Forum*, March, 1932, 177–80.

17. "A Literary Swell," *American Mercury*, March, 1929, p. 369.

18. Review of *Hawthorne*, by Newton Arvin, *Nation*, November 13, 1929, p. 554.

19. Review of *Mamba's Daughters*, by DuBose Heyward, *Forum*, April, 1929, pp. xvi–xvii.

20. Review of *A Farewell to Arms*, by Ernest Hemingway, *Forum*, 82 (December 1929), pp. vii–xx.

21. "The World of Ernest Hemingway," *New Freeman*, 1 (March 22, 1930), 40–42.

22. "David Graham Phillips: Journalist," *Bookman*, 73 (May, 1931), 264–66.

23. "The Past and Future of William Faulkner," *Bookman*, 74 (September, 1931), 22–24.

24. "Conrad After Five Years," *New Republic*, January 8, 1930, pp. 192–94.

25. Review of *The New American Caravan*, ed. Alfred Kreymbourg et al., *Hound and Horn*, 3 (1930), 278–80.

26. Review of *Look Homeward, Angel*, by Thomas Wolfe, *New Freeman*, 1 (April 5, 1930), pp. 93–94.

27. "Ford Madox Ford—A Neglected Contemporary," *Bookman*, 72 (December, 1930), 370.

Chapter Three

1. "How I Came to Communism," *New Masses*, September, 1932, p. 8.
2. Review of *The Coming Struggle for Power*, by John Strachey, *New Masses*, October 22, 1935, pp. 26–27.
3. "The Urbanity of Mr. Krutch," *New Masses*, October 23, 1934, pp. 23–24.
4. Review of *A Yankee Saint*, by Robert A. Parker, *New Masses*, February 4, 1936, p. 27.
5. Review of *Eyeless in Gaza*, by Aldous Huxley, *New Masses*, July 21, 1936, pp. 23–24.
6. "Sinclair Lewis and the Good Life," *English Journal*, 25 (April, 1936), 265–73.
7. Review of *It Can't Happen Here*, by Sinclair Lewis, *New Masses*, October 29, 1935, pp. 22–23.
8. "The Menace to Culture," *New Masses*, April 7, 1936, p. 29.
9. Review of *Abinger Harvest*, by E. M. Forster, *New Masses*, July 7, 1936, pp. 25–26.
10. "Revaluing Ford Madox Ford," *New Masses*, April 27, 1937, p. 22.
11. *I Like America*, (New York, 1938), especially p. 148.
12. "What Can I Do?" *New Masses*, August 30, 1938, pp. 19–20.
13. Review of *Seeds of Tomorrow*, by Mikhail Sholokhov, *New Masses*, November 26, 1935, pp. 22–23.
14. "The Threat of Frustration," *New Masses*, June 15, 1937, pp. 16–18. This is a printing of the speech he made.
15. "John Dos Passos," *Bookman*, 78 (April, 1932), 32–42; review of *In All Countries*, by John Dos Passos, *New Masses*, April 24, 1934, pp. 25–26; and the following reviews, all in *New Masses*: review of *The Land of Plenty*, by Robert Cantwell, May 8, 1934, pp. 25–26; of *The Treasure of the Sierra Madre*, by B. Traven, July 16, 1935, p. 23; of *A Stone Came Rolling*, by Fielding Burke, December 3, 1935, p. 23; of *A Sign for Cain*, by Grace Lumpkin, November 12, 1935, p. 23; of *The Chute*, by Albert Halper November 23, 1937, pp. 20–21; of *Uncle Tom's Children*, by Richard Wright, March 29, 1938, pp. 23–24; and of *The Grapes of Wrath*, by John Steinbeck, May 2, 1939, pp. 22–24. All the *New Masses* reviews above except on B. Traven and Grace Lumpkin are reprinted in *Granville Hicks in the New Masses*, ed. Jack Allan Robbins (Port Washington, N.Y., 1974).
16. "Literature and Revolution," *English Journal* (college edition), 24 (March, 1935), 24.
17. Review of *Death in the Afternoon*, by Ernest Hemingway, *Nation*, November 9, 1932, p. 461; review of *Green Hills of Africa*, by Hem-

ingway, *New Masses*, November 19, 1935, p. 23; review of *To Have and Have Not*, by Hemingway, *New Masses*, October 26, 1937, pp. 22–23.

18. "The Case Against Willa Cather," *English Journal*, 22 (November, 1933), 704–10; review of *Joseph and His Brothers*, by Thomas Mann, *New Masses*, June 19, 1934, p. 25; review of *Pylon*, by William Faulkner, *New Masses*, May 14, 1935, p. 25; review of *The Years*, by Virginia Woolf, *New Republic*, April 28, 1937, p. 363.

19. Review of *The Plebian's Progress*, by Frank Tilsley, *Nation*, September 13, 1933, pp. 305–6; "Granville Hicks Comments" (on Andre Malraux), *New Masses*, September 4, 1934, pp. 29–30; review of *Love on the Dole*, by Walter Greenwood, *New Masses*, September 4, 1934, p. 25; review of *The Time Is Ripe*, by Greenwood, *New Masses*, April 2, 1935, p. 33.

20. "Those Who Quibble, Bicker, Nag, and Deny," review of *New Letters in America*, ed. Horace Gregory, *New Masses*, September 28, 1937, pp. 22–23.

21. " 'Good News' in American Literature, A Symposium," *New Masses*, October 12, 1937, pp. 18–19.

22. "The Collective Novel," *Anvil*, September–October, 1933, pp. 7–8.

23. "The Mystery of the Best Seller," *English Journal*, 23 (October, 1934), 626–29.

24. The following summaries and quotes are from "Revolution and the Novel: Parts 1–7, " *New Masses*, April 3, 1934, pp. 29–31; April 10, pp. 23–25; April 17, pp. 24–25; April 24, pp. 23–25; May 8, pp. 22–24; May 15, pp. 23–25; and May 22, pp. 23–25. Like most of the pieces from the *New Masses*, this series is reprinted in *Granville Hicks in the New Masses*, ed. Jack Alan Robbins.

25. *The Great Tradition*, rev. ed. (New York, 1935), p. 329. First edition (1933) ends with a similar statement, pp. 305–6.

26. Regarding the controversy surrounding the Hicks biography of Reed, see *Part of the Truth*, pp. 141–42 and 165–68, and the bibliography of this book, under "Selected Articles" by Hicks.

27. *Part of the Truth*, p. 150.

Chapter Four

1. "Literary Criticism and the Marxian Method," *Modern Quarterly*, 6 (Summer, 1932), 44–47.

2. "An Open Letter," *New Masses*, January 2, 1934, p. 24.

3. "The Crisis in American Criticism," *New Masses*, February 8, 1933, pp. 3–5; see also "Literature and Revolution," *English Journal*, (college ed.), 24 (March, 1935), 219–39, and "The Social Interpretation of Literature," *Progressive Education*, 11 (January, 1934), 49–54.

4. *The Great Tradition*, pp. 205–6.

5. Review of *The Liberation of American Literature*, by V. F. Calverton, *New Republic*, September 7, 1932, pp. 104–5.

6. "Assumptions in Literature," *Engish Journal*, 25 (November, 1936), 709–17.

7. "Proust and the Proletariat," *New Masses*, November 20, 1934, pp. 21–22.

8. Review of *Vachel Lindsay*, by Edgar Lee Masters, *New Masses*, December 24, 1935, p. 26.

9. Review of *To Have and Have Not*, by Ernest Hemingway, *New Masses*, October 26, 1937, pp. 22–23.

10. *The Great Tradition* revised edition of 1935 is identical to the 1933 edition down to p. 292. In the revised edition, Hicks ended chapter 8 on that page and added a chapter 11 about the then recent revolutionary literature in America.

11. *Figures of Transition* (New York, 1939), p. 108; references to this book will be indicated by page numbers in the text.

Chapter Five

1. *Part of the Truth*, p. 176.

2. "A Communication: On Leaving the Communist Party," *New Republic*, October 4, 1939, pp. 244–45.

3. "The Blind Alley of Marxism," *Nation*, September 28, 1940, pp. 264–67.

4. "The Failure of Left Criticism," *New Republic*, September 9, 1940, pp. 345–47.

5. Foreword to paperback reprint of *The Great Tradition* (Chicago, 1969), p. x.

6. Afterword to reprint of *The Great Tradition*, pp. 308–9.

7. Ibid., p. 310.

8. Ibid., pp. 311–12.

9. Ibid., pp. 313–14 on James; p. 318 on Frost.

10. Ibid., p. 319. Hicks mentions other authors as well: Thornton Wilder, Ernest Hemingway, and John Dos Passos, for example, pp. 319–21.

11. "On Attitudes and Ideas," *Partisan Review*, 5 (March–April, 1947), 117–29.

12. "Communism," in *New International Yearbook* (New York, 1946–1958).

13. "The Spectre That Haunts the World," *Harper's*, 192 (June, 1946), 536–42.

14. "The Liberals Who Haven't Learned," *Commentary*, 11 (April, 1951), 319–29.

15. "Is McCarthyism a Phantom?" *New Leader*, June 4, 1951, p. 7.

16. *Where We Came Out* (New York, 1954), pp. 243–44; also p. 19.

17. "Communism and the American Intellectual," in *Whose Revolution?* ed. Irving DeWitt Talmadge (New York, 1941), 78–115.

18. "Lincoln Steffens: He Covered the Future," *Commentary*, 8 (February, 1952), 147–55.

19. Review of *The Quest for Utopia*, by Glenn Negley and J. Max Patrick, *New Leader*, April 21, 1952, pp. 22–23.

20. Review of *White Collar*, by C. Wright Mills, *New Leader*, January 28, 1952, pp. 24–25.

21. "A Discussion of 'Intransigent Radicalism' and 'Critical Liberalism,' " *New Leader*, February 8, 1954, pp. 22–23.

22. Review of *The Hound of Earth*, by Vance Bourjaily, *New Leader*, February 28, 1955, pp. 21–22.

23. "Imagination and the End We Seek," review of *A Continuing Journey*, by Archibald MacLeish, *Saturday Review*, January 27, 1968, pp. 23–24.

24. *Harvard Class of 1923 Fiftieth Anniversary Report* (Cambridge, 1973), 246–48.

25. Terry Long, "Interview with Granville Hicks," *Antioch Review*, 33 (Summer, 1975), 93–102.

Chapter Six

1. *The First To Awaken* (New York, 1940), p. 341.

2. *Only One Storm* (New York, 1942), p. 412.

3. Ibid., p. 414.

4. This information comes from a conversation I had with Hicks on October 5, 1974.

5. *There Was a Man in Our Town* (New York, 1952), p. 281.

6. *Small Town* (New York, 1946), p. 36; references to this book appear by page number in the text.

7. "Roxborough, Post-Truman," *Commentary*, 15 (March, 1953), p. 235.

8. "Jacques Barzun Examines America—Its Techniques, Its Culture, Its Values," *New Leader*, May 10, 1954, pp. 11–12; review of *This Demi-Paradise*, by Margaret Halsey, *Saturday Review*, July 30, 1960, p. 12.

9. Review of *Big Dreams in a Small Town and What Time Did To Them*, by Edwin Roskam, *New York Times Book Review*, July 30, 1972, pp. 7, 13.

10. Review of *A Nation of Strangers*, by Vance Packard, *New York Times Book Review*, September 10, 1972, pp. 2–3, 50–51.

Chapter Seven

1. "Literature in This Global War," *College English*, 4 (May, 1943), 453–59.

2. "The Shape of Postwar Literature," *College English*, 5 (May, 1944), 407–12.

3. "The Ground Alfred Kazin Stands On," *Antioch Review*, 4 (Spring, 1943), 21–31.

4. Review of *Bernard Clare*, by James T. Farrell; *The American*, by Howard Fast; and *All the King's Men*, by Robert Penn Warren, *American Mercury*, 63 (October, 1946), 494–500.

5. "New Literary Editor Comes to Defense of Book Reviewers and Book Reviewing," *New Leader*, November 12, 1951, pp. 20–21.

6. "The Enemies of Literature," *New Leader*, May 5, 1952, pp. 17–18.

7. Review of *Stephen Crane: An Omnibus*, by R. W. Stallman, and *The Days Before*, by Katherine Anne Porter, *New Leader*, December 29, 1952, pp. 21–22.

8. "The State of Literary Journalism: Is the Serious Novel Expendable?" *New Leader*, December 10, 1956, pp. 8–10.

9. "Some Literary Fallacies," *English Journal*, 33 (November, 1944), 461–65.

10. Review of *The Confident Years*, by Van Wyck Brooks, *New Leader*, January 14, 1952, pp. 20–21.

11. Reviews of *The Writer in America*, by Brooks, and *The Forlorn Demon*, by Allen Tate, *New Leader*, April 27, 1953, pp. 21–22.

12. "Mr. Hicks Launches New Feature With Discussion of Edmund Wilson," *New Leader*, December 1, 1952, pp. 20–21.

13. "American Fiction Since the War," *English Journal*, 27 (June, 1948), 271–77.

14. "The Best American Novels Since 1945," *New Leader*, December 14, 1953, pp. 12–14.

15. "Fiction Chronicle: Novels by Halevy, Ellison, Bonner, Gallagher and Goyen," *New Leader*, August 1, 1955, pp. 15–16.

16. "The State of Literary Journalism," p. 9.

17. Review of *Selected Writings of William Dean Howells*, ed. Henry Steele Commager, *Sewanee Review*, 59 (Summer, 1951), 505–17.

18. "Fiction and Social Criticism," *College English*, 13 (April, 1952), 355–61.

19. "John Phillips, Oakley Hall, Allan Seager Speak Up for Our Dissatisfied Youth," *New Leader*, May 18, 1953, pp. 13–14.

20. Review of *The Dollmaker*, by Harriette Arnow, *New Leader*, April 26, 1954, p. 24.

21. "1955's Young Novelists Say Farewell To Old Timidity on Social Themes," *New Leader*, December 12, 1955, pp. 9–11.

22. "In a Novel It's the Life, Not the Politics, That Counts," *New York Times Book Review*, August 12, 1956, p. 5.

23. Review of *Politics and the Novel*, by Irving Howe, *New Leader*, March 11, 1957, pp. 23–24.

24. "The Novel Isn't Dying," *New Leader*, December 10, 1951, pp. 23–24.

25. *The Living Novel, A Symposium* (New York, 1957), 212–24.

26. Review of *Some Corner of An English Field*, by Dannie Abse, *New Leader*, January 28, 1957, p. 22.

27. Review of *The Return of Ansel Gibbs*, by Frederick Buechner, *New Leader*, February 24, 1958, p. 20.

28. Review of *Bread from Heaven*, by Henrietta Buckmaster, *Commentary*, 14 (November, 1952), 512–13.

29. Review of *The Crack in the Column*, by Anthony Weller, *Tomorrow*, 9 (December, 1949), 57–58.

30. Review of *The Black Prince*, by Shirley Ann Grau, *New Leader*, January 31, 1955, p. 23.

31. Review of *East of Eden*, by John Steinbeck, and *The Center of the Stage*, by Gerald Sykes, *New Leader*, September 29, 1952, pp. 21–22.

32. Review of *The Wars of Love*, by Mark Schorer and other novels, *New Leader*, March 15, 1954, pp. 17–18.

33. Review of *By Love Possessed*, by James Gould Cozzens, *New Leader*, September 2, 1957, pp. 17–18.

34. "Dos Passos and His Critics," *American Mercury*, 27 (June, 1948), 271–77; for a discussion of Dos Passos as a satirist, see Charles T. Ludington, Jr., "The Neglected Satires of John Dos Passos," *Satire Newsletter* 7 (1970), 127–36.

35. "Marquand of Newburyport," *Harper's*, 200 (April, 1950), 101–8.

36. "P-N Fiction," *College English*, 13 (December, 1946), 107–12.

37. "Some Literary Detective Work," *New Leader*, November 19, 1951, pp. 20–21.

38. "Faulkner's South, A Northern Interpretation," *Georgia Review*, Fall, 1951, 269–84.

39. Review of *William Faulkner: A Critical Study*, by Irving Howe, *New Leader*, August 4, 1952, pp. 20–21.

40. Review of *The Town*, by William Faulkner, *New Leader*, May 13, 1957, pp. 6–8.

41. "Eudora Welty," *English Journal*, 41 (November, 1952), 461–68.

42. Review of *Sweet Thursday*, by John Steinbeck, *New Leader*, June 21, 1954, p. 25.

43. Review of *The New Men*, by C. P. Snow, *New Leader*, January 17, 1955, pp. 22–23.

44. Review of *A Walk on the Wild Side*, by Nelson Algren, *New Leader*, May 28, 1956, pp. 23–24.

45. Review of *Some Came Running*, by James Jones, *New Leader*, January 27, 1958, pp. 20–22.

Chapter Eight

1. "The Quest in a Quiet Time," *Saturday Review*, November 28, 1959, p. 20.

2. "As Fiction Faces the Sixties," *Saturday Review*, January 2, 1960, p. 14.

3. "On the Threshold of the Enduring," review of *After Alienation: American Novels in Mid-Century*, by Marcus Klein, *Saturday Review*, July 4, 1964, pp. 21–22.

4. "Signatures to the Significance of Self," *Saturday Review*, August 29, 1964, pp. 70, 72.

5. Review of *The Arrangement*, by Elia Kazan, *Saturday Review*, March 4, 1967, pp. 25–26.

6. "The Changing Novel," *Eighth Journal of the Otto Rank Society*, 5 (June, 1970), 7–18.

7. "The American Novel," *American Way*, January, 1975, pp. 17–21, published by American Airlines.

8. "Literary Horizons," *Saturday Review*, April 5, 1958, p. 14.

9. Review of *In Search of Character*, by Graham Greene, *Saturday Review*, January 6, 1962, p. 62.

10. "Art Lost in Analysis," *Saturday Review*, May 13, 1967, pp. 29–30.

11. Review of *My Enemy's Enemy*, by Kingsley Amis, *Saturday Review*, April 6, 1963, pp. 22–23.

12. Review of *I Am Mary Dunne*, by Brian Moore, *Saturday Review*, June 15, 1968, pp. 23–24; and review of *Knights and Dragons*, by Elizabeth Spencer, *Saturday Review*, June 26, 1965, p. 26.

13. Review of *End of a War*, by Edward Loomis, *Saturday Review*, April 19, 1958, p. 18.

14. Review of *The Pistol*, by James Jones, *Saturday Review*, January 10, 1959, p. 12; review of *The Patriots*, by James Barlow, and *The Trend Is Up*, by Anthony West, *Saturday Review*, September 3, 1960, p. 16.

15. Review of *From the Terrace*, by John O'Hara, *Saturday Review*, November 29, 1958, p. 14.

16. Review of *The Power of Blackness*, by Harry Levin, *Saturday Review*, April 26, 1958, p. 12.

17. Review of *The Exiles*, by Albert Guerard, *Saturday Review*, February 9, 1963, p. 26.

18. "'Breakfast of Champions' and Other Madness," a review of novels by John Cheever, Bernard Malamud, Philip Roth and Kurt Vonnegut, Jr., *American Way*, August, 1973, p. 14.

19. Review of *The Collector*, by John Fowles, *Saturday Review*, July 27, 1963, pp. 19–20.

20. Review of *The Comedians*, by Graham Greene, *Saturday Review*, January 29, 1966, pp. 35–36.

21. "The Importance of People," review of *The Middle Age of Mrs. Eliot*, by Angus Wilson, *Saturday Review*, March 21, 1959, p. 22.

22. Review of *Corridors of Power*, by C. P. Snow, *Saturday Review*, September 12, 1964, p. 33.

23. Review of *The Benefactor*, by Susan Sontag, *Saturday Review*, September 7, 1963, pp. 17–18.

24. Review of *Come Back, Dr. Caligari*, by Donald Barthelme, *Saturday Review*, April 4, 1964, pp. 23–24.

25. Review of *Crybaby of the Western World*, by John Leonard; *Nog*, by Rudolph Wurlitzer; and *Rose*, by Marilyn Hoff, *Saturday Review*, March 22, 1969, p. 54.

26. "As Fiction Faces the Sixties," p. 14.

27. "The Personality Paradox," review of *Casanova's Chinese Restaurant*, by Anthony Powell, *Saturday Review*, October 22, 1960, p. 16.

28. "Generations of the Fifties: Malamud, Gold, and Updike," in *The Creative Present*, ed. Nona Balakian and Charles Simmons (Garden City, N.Y., 1963), pp. 213–37.

29. "1966: The Reviewer Reviews," *Saturday Review*, December 31, 1966, pp. 17–18.

30. Review of *The Reivers*, by William Faulkner, *Saturday Review*, June 2, 1962, p. 27.

31. Review of *Faulkner*, ed. Robert Penn Warren, *Saturday Review*, May 6, 1967, pp. 27–28.

32. "A Feeling About Life" (on the death of Ernest Hemingway), *Saturday Review*, July 29, 1961, pp. 30, 38.

33. Review of *Theophilus North*, by Thornton Wilder, *New York Times Book Review*, October 21, 1973, pp. 1, 16.

34. "Behind the Gatsby Phenomenon," *American Way*, May, 1974, pp. 14–18.

35. "Introduction," in *Wright Morris: A Reader* (New York, 1970), pp. ix–xxxiii.

36. Review of *The Magic Barrel*, by Bernard Malamud, *Saturday Review*, May 17, 1958, p. 10. This and the following reviews are all reprinted in Hicks's book *Literary Horizons* (New York, 1970), pp. 65–83.

37. Review of *A New Life*, by Bernard Malamud, *Saturday Review*, October 7, 1961, p. 20.

38. Review of *The Fixer*, by Bernard Malamud, *Saturday Review*, September 10, 1966, pp. 37–39.

39. Foreword to Bernard Malamud section, *Literary Horizons: A Quarter Century of American Fiction* (New York, 1970), p. 65.

40. Foreword to Saul Bellow section, *Literary Horizons*, p. 49.

41. Review of *The Adventures of Augie March*, by Saul Bellow, *New Leader*, September 21, 1953, pp. 23–24; reprinted in *Literary Horizons*, pp. 51–53, as are the following reviews.

42. Review of *Henderson the Rain King*, by Saul Bellow, *Saturday Review*, February 21, 1959, p. 20.

43. Review of *Herzog*, by Saul Bellow, *Saturday Review*, September 19, 1964, pp. 37–38.

44. Afterword on Bellow, *Literary Horizons*, p. 63.

45. Review of *Humboldt's Gift*, by Saul Bellow, *American Way*, November, 1975, p. 40. This is not reprinted in *Literary Horizons*.

46. "They Needn't Say No," *Saturday Review*, July 2, 1960, p. 14; and review of *Advertisements for Myself*, by Norman Mailer, *Saturday Review*, November 7, 1959, p. 18.

47. Review of *An American Dream*, by Norman Mailer, *Saturday Review*, March 20, 1965, pp. 23–24.

48. Afterword on Philip Roth, *Literary Horizons*, p. 255.

49. "A Matter of Critical Opinion," *Saturday Review*, August 7, 1965, pp. 19–20.

50. Review of *Why Are We in Vietnam?*, by Norman Mailer, *Saturday Review*, September 16, 1967, pp. 39–40; this and all reviews above are reprinted in the book *Literary Horizons*.

51. *Literary Horizons*, pp. 259–72, on John Barth.

52. Ibid, pp. 109–33; and review of *A Month of Sundays*, by John Updike, *American Way*, April, 1975, pp. 56–58.

53. *Literary Horizons*, pp. 209–23, on Vladimir Nabokov.

54. Ibid., pp. 85–105, on James Baldwin.

55. Ibid., pp. 245–55, on Philip Roth.

56. Ibid., pp. 151–71, on Herbert Gold.

57. Ibid., pp. 229–42, on Reynolds Price.

58. Ibid., pp. 227–28, and review of *Something Happened*, by Joseph Heller, *American Way*, November, 1974, pp. 37–38.

59. *Literary Horizons*, pp. 173–83; and review of *Breakfast of Champions*, by Kurt Vonnegut, Jr., *American Way*, August, 1973, p. 14.

60. Review of *The Crying of Lot 49*, by Thomas Pynchon, *Saturday Review*, April 30, 1966, pp. 27–28.

61. Review of *Nickel Mountain*, by John Gardner, *American Way*, July, 1974, pp. 38–39.

Chapter Nine

1. Morton D. Zabel, ed., *Literary Opinion in America*, 3d ed. rev. (Gloucester, Mass.: 1968), foreword to the Torchbook Edition, 1962, pp. xviii–xix.

2. Zabel, "Introduction: Criticism in America," *Literary Opinion in America*, ibid., p. 40.

Selected Bibliography

1. Books

Eight Ways of Looking at Christianity. New York: Macmillan, 1928.
The Great Tradition: An Interpretation of American Literature Since the Civil War. New York: Macmillan, 1933; rev. ed., 1935; reprint ed., paperback, Chicago: Quadrangle, 1969. Reprint includes new foreword and afterword by Hicks.
Proletarian Literature in the United States. Edited by Granville Hicks, Michael Gold, Isidor Schneider, Joseph North, Paul Peters, and Alan Calmer. New York: International Publishers, 1935.
One of Us: The Story of John Reed. New York: Equinox Cooperative Press, 1935. Small picture book; narrative by Hicks.
John Reed: The Making of a Revolutionary. New York: Macmillan, 1936. Concerning a controversy later over this biography, see "Setting the Record Straight on an Episode in the Red Decade" and "Playboy Poet to Revolutionary," both listed below under essays by Hicks.
I Like America. New York: Modern Age Books, 1938. Hicks advocates communism for America.
The *Letters of Lincoln Steffens.* Edited by Hicks and Ella Winter. New York: Harcourt, Brace, 1938. Brief introductions by editors.
Figures of Transition: A Study of British Literature at the End of the Nineteenth Century. New York: Macmillan, 1939. Hicks's second (and better) attempt at a Marxist interpretation of literary history.
The First To Awaken. New York: Modern Age Books, 1940. Novel about the year 2040, a creditable utopian fiction.
Only One Storm. New York: Macmillan, 1942. Novel about politically liberal man who moves his family back to his New England hometown.
Behold Trouble. New York: Macmillan, 1944. Novel about the reactions of a New York village to a conscientious objector; vigorously narrated: Hicks's best fictional work.
Small Town. New York: Macmillan, 1946. Informal social study of fictional town Roxborough, based on Grafton, New York.
There Was A Man in Our Town. New York: Viking, 1952. Novel about the impact of a New York village on a sociologist.
Where We Came Out. New York: Viking, 1954. Discussion of the appeal

of communism in the 1930s, its dangers in the Cold War years, the wrongness of McCarthyism, and social changes in America.

The Living Novel. Edited by Granville Hicks. New York: Macmillan, 1957. Introduction by Hicks, with essays by Wright Morris, Ralph Ellison, Saul Bellow, and others.

Part of the Truth. New York: Harcourt, Brace and World, 1965. Hicks's autobiography.

James Gould Cozzens. Minnesota Pamphlets on American Literature. Minneapolis: University of Minnesota Press, 1966. Important study of Cozzens, with emphasis on value of *By Love Possessed.*

Literary Horizons: A Quarter Century of American Fiction. Edited by Jack Alan Robbins. New York: New York University Press, 1970. Collection of reviews Hicks did in the 1950s and 1960s. with new forewords and afterwords. Authors covered: Wright Morris, Saul Bellow, Bernard Malamud, James Baldwin, John Updike, Flannery O'Connor, Herbert Gold, Kurt Vonnegut, Louis Auchincloss, Vladimir Nabokov, Joseph Heller, Reynolds Price, Philip Roth, John Barth, and Norman Mailer.

Granville Hicks in the New Masses. Edited by Jack Alan Robbins. Port Washington, N.Y.: Kennikat, 1974. A well-edited collection of Hicks's writings in the 1930s, with useful historical notes.

2. Selected Articles

"Arnold Toynbee: The Boldest Historian." *Harper's*, 194 (February, 1947), 116–24.

"As Fiction Faces the Sixties." *Saturday Review*, January 2, 1960, p. 14.

"Art Lost in Analysis." *Saturday Review*, May 13, 1967, pp. 29–30.

"Blind Alley of Marxism, The." *Nation*, September 28, 1940, pp. 264–67.

"Failure of Left Criticism, The." *New Republic*, September 9, 1940, pp. 345–47.

"Fiction and Social Criticism." *College English*, 13 (April, 1952), 355–61.

"Fighting Decade, The." *Saturday Review*, July 6, 1940, pp. 3–5, 16–17. Statement on the radical 1930s and the end of an era.

"How Red Was the Red Decade?" *Harper's*, 207 (July, 1953), 53–61.

"Is McCarthyism a Phantom?" *New Leader*, June 4, 1951, p. 7. Criticism of McCarthyism but wariness toward Communists as well.

"Liberals Who Haven't Learned, The." *Commentary*, 11 (April, 1951), 319–29. About liberals who still tend to give Russia the benefit of every doubt.

"On Attitudes and Ideas." *Partisan Review*, 5 (March–April, 1947), 117–29. A cogent statement on the problems and pitfalls of radical politics, part of a series on "The Future of Socialism."

"Playboy Poet to Revolutionary." *Saturday Review*, November 4, 1967, pp. 29–30. Review of *The Lost Revolutionary: A Biography of John Reed*, by Richard O'Connor and Dale Walker. Reviewing a newer biography of Reed, Hicks disagrees with authors that Reed was sour on communism when he died in Russia or that Reed's partisanship interfered with his reporting in *Ten Days That Shook the World*.

"Quest in a Quiet Time, The." *Saturday Review*, November 28, 1959, p. 20. On novelists in the 1950s.

"Re-Reading of *Moby Dick*." In *Twelve Original Essays on Great American Novels*. Edited by Charles Shapiro, pp. 44–68. Detroit: Wayne State University Press, 1958. A useful discussion of Melville's novel.

"Setting the Record Straight on an Episode in the Red Decade." *New Leader*, June 15, 1953, pp. 20–22. Hicks defends himself against a statement in a letter by Sherwood Anderson that he covered up John Reed's souring on communism in the Reed biography. Quotes a letter he has from Anderson praising the biography at the time.

"Signatures to the Significance of the Self." *Saturday Review*, August 29, 1964, pp. 67, 70, 72. On the value of fiction.

"The Spectre That Haunts the World." *Harper's*, 192 (June, 1946), 536–42. Analysis of the rise of communism and its being centered in Russia; need for push for social justice by non-Communist nations.

"The State of Literary Journalism: Is the Serious Novel Expendable?" *New Leader*, December 10, 1956, pp. 8–10.

"Whitaker Chambers's Testament." *New Leader*, May 26, 1952, pp. 19–22. Review of *Witness*. Qualified admiration for Chambers and belief by Hicks that Alger Hiss was guilty.

3. Letters and Private Papers

Syracuse University has the Hicks private papers through 1965, including all letters. All his papers are to be deposited there eventually. His reports as a publisher's reader for Macmillan are included. The letters include correspondence between Hicks and Newton Arvin. Copies of the Hicks-Arvin letters are also on file at Smith College.

SECONDARY SOURCES

1. Critical Commentary

Few essays of any length have been written about Hicks. Scattered comments in various books about American literature and about the Depression era mention him in passing, especially concerning his mistakes as a Marxist critic. The following are the most salient:

AARON, DANIEL. "The Arrival and Departure of Granville Hicks." In *Writers on the Left: Episodes in American Literary Communism*. New York: Harcourt, Brace & World, 1961. Pp. 354–64. Index has other references to Hicks. A chapter of the book, describing briefly

Hicks's attraction to communism, his defense of it, and his disillusionment with it.

COWLEY, MALCOLM. *Think Back on Us . . . A Contemporary Chronicle of the 1930's.* Carbondale: Southern Illinois University Press, 1967. Collection of *New Republic* essays; Hicks discussed on pp. 47–51, 78–80, and 112–115. Cowley is basically sympathetic but offers some criticisms of Hicks, too.

"Granville Hicks." *Current Biography*, 3, no. 5 (May, 1942), pp. 44–46. Facts of his life up to 1942.

HOOK, SIDNEY. "Myths of Marx." *Saturday Review*, May 15, 1954, pp. 11–12. A review of Hicks's *Where We Came Out*, with sympathy and understanding.

KAUFFMANN, STANLEY. "Youth in the Thirties." *New Republic*, September 18, 1965, pp. 17–20. A sneering review of Hicks's autobiography, *Part of the Truth*, comparing it unfavorably with Alfred Kazin's *Starting Out in the Thirties.*

KAZIN, ALFRED. *On Native Grounds.* New York: Harcourt, Brace and World, 1942. On Marxist critics of the 1930s, pp. 417–24, including Hicks.

———. *Starting Out in the Thirties.* Boston: Little, Brown, 1962. Pp. 145–46. Mentions Hicks condescendingly.

SLATER, JOSEPH. "A Pattern of Days and Ideas." *Saturday Review*, July 31, 1965, pp. 18–19. Review of Hicks's autobiography, praising it.

2. Academic Studies

BICKER, ROBERT J. *Granville Hicks: An Annotated Bibliography.* Emporia, Kansas: Emporia State Research Studies, 1968. Useful list covering Hicks from 1927 through June, 1968. Index of authors reviewed by Hicks. Some errors and omissions.

LONG, TERRY L. "Interview with Granville Hicks." *Antioch Review*, 33 (Summer, 1975), 93–102. Hicks answers questions about his current views on politics, literary criticism, recent authors, and the state of the world.

———. *The Radical Criticism of Granville Hicks in the 1930's.* Ann Arbor, Mich.: University Microfilms, 1972. Covers material discussed in this book in chapters 3–5, plus more on Marxist theory in general and on the social background of the 1930s.

PARRINGTON, VERNON LOUIS, JR. *American Dreams: A Study of American Utopias.* Providence, R.I.: Brown University, 1947. Pp. 211–14. Points out the basic attitudes toward government and Utopia in Hicks's novels *The First To Awaken* and *Only One Storm.*

SHERWIN, ROBERT T. *The Literary Career of Granville Hicks.* Ann Arbor, Mich.: University Microfilms, 1976. Describes the whole career of Hicks, with emphasis on his ideas about the role of the critic; argues that Hicks's greatest failing as a novelist was that his themes are "too obvious for the careful reader."

Index

171